Conversations with a Crackhead

Creating Calm in the Chaotic Mind

Rokhy Isharii

Published by Clink Street Publishing 2022

Copyright © 2022

First edition.

Text © Rokhy Isharii 2020

crackheadconversations@gmail.com

A catalogue record for this book is available from the British Library.

ISBN:
978-1-914498-23-7 - paperback
978-1-914498-24-4 - ebook

For Mum, Dad and my sister

DISCLAIMER

The information provided within this Book/eBook is for general information purposes only. Any use of the methods described are the author's personal thoughts. They are intended to be a definitive set of instructions for this project. You may discover there are other methods and materials to accomplish the same end result.

Before beginning any new exercise program it is recommended that you seek medical advice from your personal physician. This book is not intended to be a substitute for the medical advice of a licensed physician. The reader should consult with their doctor in any matters relating to his/her/they health.

The information contained within this Book/eBook is strictly for educational purposes. The information is presented as general advice on self care. If you wish to apply ideas contained in this Book/eBook, you are taking full responsibility for your actions. The author does not assume and hereby disclaims any liability to any persons for any loss or damage suffered.

Contents

PART II

Preface

This book was written in 2020. That year will forever be synonymous with the outbreak of Covid-19, although lockdown was one of the best things to ever happen for me. The creation of this book took place during my gap year, between graduating and starting a new job. I was at a low point, and the last four years felt like a huge waste of time and effort. All my expectations, my goals – graduating with a first, having a "fit" physique, a girlfriend and a graduate role – were all unticked so on 11th October 2019, I started a course in meditation and removed myself from all social media. The continuous barrage of women, six-packs, money and success wasn't something I needed to see on a daily basis from Instagram, Snapchat and Facebook. Seeing all my fellow graduates smashing life only served to remind me how far behind I was. With hindsight, I realise I wasn't so far behind, but my perception at the time was very different.

This became the catalyst for change. I began to meditate daily, sometimes twice a day and focused on thinking positively and manifesting what I wanted from life. My outlook brightened, but then after many attempts and countless rejections to get into investment banking between September 2019 and January 2020, I felt burnt out and couldn't help thinking: *Now what? I've spent all this time gearing up for this point and have nothing to show. I did everything I was supposed to and more. I prepared, thought positively, focused on my goal and still nothing.* My only salvation was writing once a week in a little café in Euston, known as the Observatory. These times became the cathartic unloading I needed to deal with my inner voice – which I call "the crackhead."

From the end of January 2020, I read a myriad of self-help books, continued meditation, changed my diet and lost 12kg (through training and diet over five months) and dove even deeper into psychodynamic therapy. I put every ounce of my energy into focusing on my internal self and, as a result, my year transformed into the best one of my life so far.

We all have a crackhead. At times it can be funny, it can excite, create expectations, increase fear and numerous other emotions. Your crackhead is as unique to you as mine is to me; it is a metamorphosis of the environment we are exposed too and something that can control us if we don't learn to recognise and live with it. That decision you regret, the choice you wish you hadn't made in anger, sadness or even happiness, is usually the crackhead's doing. How many times have you built up stories in your head about things that aren't even true, only to come face-to-face with reality and realise it is nowhere near as bad as you thought? Your crackhead is not you; it is just a part of you. Knowing that your crackhead does this, why would you trust it?

***

There are two parts to this book. Part I is a narrative told through the eyes of Kaiya and Rio. These two fictional characters share some of my personality traits (as well as those of my closest friends and family members). The events unfold over five sections, each portraying a different lesson from daily life. If you are that way inclined, you might note references to spiritual traditions, such as Buddhism and Hinduism. But this book doesn't intend to offer or preach any spiritual lessons. The titles of each section are named after five of the seven chakras (which once aligned bring balance with mental and spiritual wellbeing). The word "chakra" is Sanskrit and means "wheel" or "disk." Think of the chakras as swirling pools/disks of energy within your body of which there are seven. The narrative is structured on the chakras because when we are happy and excited, we are full of energy, but when we are sad, we feel lethargic and drained – and our thoughts affect our beliefs.

Your beliefs control your emotions and, as a result, your energy levels. If I think about something positive, I feel good and naturally want to do something. My energy levels, therefore, control what actions I take. The more you perform an action, the more it becomes a habit and habits create your behaviour. Ultimately it is your behaviour, a culmination of all your habits, actions, beliefs, energy, thoughts and emotions that dictate your reality.

Part II is a how-to guide that takes many of the practices described in the narrative, that I've adopted this year and explains them step-by-step so you can implement them to manifest change if you so choose.

If none of the stories or ideas resonates with you, that's absolutely fine, but I wrote this book with the singular intention that – no matter who you are, whatever your life stage – you can gain at least one thing from it. If this year has taught me anything, it is that no matter what is going on in life, getting some perspective on it, is what counts. **Change your thoughts, and your reality usually changes too.**

Thank you for picking up this book, I hope you enjoy reading it as much as I did writing it.

Change Your Thoughts,
Change Your Reality.

PART I

Muladhara
(Root Chakra)

EARTH

Kaiya: "It is only when we reach our lowest point that we are now open to the greatest change."

Rio: "Just because you see your insecurity doesn't mean other people do."

KAIYA

Early Doors

Have you ever wondered what it's like to have two mothers? One biological, one adopted? Well, this is my reality and never in a million years would I have imagined this.

I was born and raised in North London. The festive period had just settled in, and I was at home practising for an upcoming dance showcase. I always loved this time of the year as I had more time to rehearse my routines, but more so because I enjoyed spending time with both my parents. We were a great trinity. It was a Saturday afternoon (I can't remember the date) but I remember seeing snowflakes in the shape of crystal diamonds falling. I was so lost in the music and my routine that I didn't even realise my parents were watching me. They always loved watching me, and I loved them watching me. Mum and Dad smiled before asking me to sit down with them for an important chat. I enjoyed my alone time as I could do what I wanted. I didn't like going along with other people's plans – especially when they involved something I didn't enjoy, but my parents always reminded me that it's good to have friends around you.

"Kaiya, honey, we have something we need to talk to you about," Mum said as we sat down together on the sofa. I always sat between the two of them. We were the perfect custard cream (this is not a racially motivated remark, but rather due to my insatiable love of the aforementioned biscuits). However, on this occasion, my parents both sat opposite me.

"What is it, Mum?"

"I want you to remember that no matter what, your father and I love you very much and that will never change."

"Okay." I wasn't fully paying attention as I was still performing the final steps of the routine in my head. I could never leave my routine unfinished. I had to do this big leap in the air, but when I had leapt into the move, I couldn't remember landing. The floor disappeared, my heart was racing, and I was just falling now.

". . . divorce."

"What did you say?" My head turned slowly towards her, hoping I'd misheard.

"Your father and I have agreed to get a divorce."

"Wait, why? What happened? Did Dad do something?" I questioned this due to a girl at school being in the same situation because her dad fell in love with another woman. So, as you can imagine, I had to check. What happened next rocked me to my core and would affect me for many years to come.

"No, Kaiya, I haven't done anything," said Dad. I was still falling in my head. I got up off the sofa. I needed to move; it felt like I was sitting too close to them, so I put some distance between us.

"Then, why is this happening? Tell me the truth, I want to know!" I demanded.

"Kaiya, watch your tone," said Mum, reminding me who was who in this relationship. "Kaiya, your father and I still care for each other very much, but I have fallen in love with someone else." I could see the distress now washing over their faces, my mother's especially.

"Who is he? And I'm not calling him dad. I already hate him." I crossed my arms and turned away from them. I didn't want to look. I felt a hand on my right shoulder.

"Kaiya listen to what your mother has to say. This isn't easy for anyone." I turned around reluctantly.

"Kaiya, you don't have to call anyone anything, but her name is Sarah."

THUD! I was no longer falling; my body smacked the floor instantly, and I felt weak. I didn't want to get up. Megan had never fully accepted this part of herself until she met and fell in love with Sarah, her best friend of the last five years.

"Well, this is spectacular! My mother loves another woman. Wait till this gets out at school." I ran upstairs into my bedroom, slamming the door behind me. I put on my headphones, played my music and continued to practise dancing until my feet were sore.

***

Over time I came to hate my mother. She broke up our family – ruined everything. Of course, 50 per cent of something is better than 100 per cent of nothing, and yet at that moment, I felt like I had nothing. I was closer to my mother than to my dad. But this changed everything.

Time passed on as I grew up without that strong female figure in my life, and then one day, it happened. I ran to the toilet and didn't know what to do. My first period had arrived. I left school "sick" that day after visiting the nurse's office. I was too mortified to tell them I didn't know what I was doing, so I watched a video on the internet.

About a week later, I decided to check with the school nurse that I was doing everything the right way. My dad did his best, but it wasn't the same. We had a pick 'n' mix of tampons, pads, cotton wool, towels, etc. in the bathroom until I was confident enough to buy everything on my own. A momentous milestone in becoming a woman and my mother wasn't there to share it. I learnt very quickly that this would be the case for many milestones growing up.

Meet the Gang

Megan moved out of the house within a week of that fateful conversation. It was official. It was just Batman and Robin, Rodney and DelBoy, Dad and I. From the age of eleven to eighteen, I saw Megan no more than five times – the last time was on my sixteenth birthday. Even though Dad and I were such a good duo, I often felt lonely as he mostly worked away from home. My grandparents lived abroad in the US and South Africa, so I didn't see them unless we were on holiday. I was about fourteen when Dad taught me how to cook, about the same time, he started travelling a lot for business. I loved his homemade prawn curry and his eggs *a la Rahul,* so naturally, these were the first two dishes I learnt to cook. It was nice though having the house to myself. It gave me a real sense of independence and taught me not to rely on anybody.

I used to let my friends stay over when Dad was away and pretend to have adult dinner parties. We would spend the night casting aspersions on all the other kids at school. There was one night in particular where they were picking on a boy named Rio in my Design Technology class. I never liked verbally assaulting Rio or anyone else for that matter. Rio had a sense of humour that came across as quite dry, but he made me laugh. However, there were many occasions where he would be as miserable as a wet weekend. Above all though, he always asked how I was feeling, which nobody else at school really did. On this night in particular, we were all sitting on my double bed watching a film.

"Did you see Rio get wound up again today? That boy obsesses over his height way too much," Ikari[1] (pronounced *ik-R-i*) said, interrupting the film.

"Well, I would feel like that if I was the average height of a girl," laughed Fuan[2] (pronounced *fu-An*).

---

1   *Ikari* = anger (Japanese)

2   *Fuan* = anxiety (Japanese)

"Girls, can we not bitch about him for once, he isn't that bad." Oh shit… I just put my foot in it. As soon as I said it, I knew I would regret it. Ikari paused the film, and all the noise fell from the room, leaving me the sole centre of attention as they circled around me.

"Oh my God, Kaiya, you like him, don't you?" Ikari stated. I didn't like Rio. OK, that's a lie. Sometimes I found him attractive, other times I didn't. It was a very confusing time…

"Aww, look at how cute she is, she's blushing now," Fuan said sarcastically.

"Chill out, I've seen him checking me out too so don't think you're anything special, Kaiya," said Hihan[3] (*pronounced hi-hAn*), ensuring she wasn't left out of the conversation.

I began to feel hot all of a sudden. My breathing became shallower, and nausea hit me like a brick wall. The lump in my throat was so engorged I found it hard to swallow. I had three gargoyles staring directly at me now. What do I say? Crap, the fourth one is about to say something.

"Kaiya, you'll be a social reject if you're with him, but more importantly a taller girl with a smaller guy doesn't look right now, does it? What are you going to tell us next? You like that girl Ashley too, and you want to be like your mother?" said Asveekaar[4] (pronounced *us-V-car*).

I swallowed my voice, laughed away my tears and said, "You're all so right, they're both just friends, but that's it. Plus, Rio is helping me get an A in DT, so that's all he is good for anyway."

"Well, make sure it stays that way. Don't be like your mother. The world doesn't accept same-sex couples. Imagine how your dad would feel if you betrayed him like that too. Make sure you don't inflict that upon yourself. After all, we're the ones who have been here for you all this time." The four gargoyles looked as satisfied as vampires after killing their prey. I could tell they were all getting off on this. They felt good. I didn't.

---

3   *Hihan* = judgement/criticism (Japanese)
4   *Asveekaar* = rejection (Hindi)

The girls you have just had the pleasure of being introduced to were some of the nastiest pieces of work I had ever met in my life, but they ended up becoming some of my best friends. I remember them picking on a girl in school, and it drew me into their crowd. Their gravitational pull was as strong as a black hole. I became drawn to their negativity, and it was addictive. I wanted to stop, but I couldn't. They showed me how to remove my own pain by being an awful human being to someone else. It helped knowing I wasn't the only person going through turbulent times. (I knew other people were going through crap, but it made me feel better to remind them of that.) The more horrible I was, the more addictive it became. But at the same time, the four girls would also keep me in my place, and this pain was also so addictive. I felt adrenaline pump through me, fear surged through my body like lightning, and I loved the sensation, even the times I felt like crying. (This has helped me understand how BDSM is a kink because pain and pleasure are so intricately linked in the brain – but that's a story for another day.)

I had lived with this type of pain for so long that I no longer knew how to live without it. It was a part of me. However, when I entered my final year of school, things started changing. I began to get tired of it all, and so when I was made to feel worthless, I didn't get my usual hit of dopamine. It had slowly been wearing off over the years, and now I felt more stuck than anything. If I upset them, they made me feel like an outcast, and I had just dedicated the better part of the last four years to being essentially a bully, and now they were the only people who would accept me.

If Dad knew what I was like at school, he would have been appalled. I have heard it said, we are the sum of our five closest friends, but the truth of it didn't dawn on me until near the end of my education. I hate to think the person I might have become if things hadn't changed as I got older. One thing stuck with me from that night, and that Asveekaar was right: I couldn't accept my mother for liking girls.

The Incident

I was paired with Sveekaar[5] (Asveekaar's twin brother, but he wasn't an asshole) and Ashley in English Literature. The three of us were working on a round table, and Ashely caught me staring at her a couple of times and vice versa. Sveekaar also noticed our exchanges but kept it to himself.

Ashley asked, "Who has the other half?"

"What do you mean?"

"Of your necklace, it looks like half of the heart is missing, or did it come like that?" Ashley said, pointing at my neck.

"It was a present from my parents. Leave it, we need to finish this piece of work." The two of them looked startled, and thankfully the bell rang, and the class was over. Sveekaar suggested that the three of us reconvene at a café after school to finish our work. I reluctantly agreed. Work had to be done.

The café was very busy, but the three of us liked working together, and I felt I could relax with them. There was a different atmosphere than when I was with the other four. We were joking and laughing when all of a sudden Sveekaar noticed Megan and Sarah walk in together.

"Isn't that your mum, Kaiya?" Sveekaar asked. I felt that lump thicken instantly, my heart began racing, and my palms became clammy, but nevertheless, I turned around to have a look. Megan had a huge smile on her face, she was holding hands with Sarah, and the two of them simply got their coffees and left. The local barista knew their order and who they were, and I heard them say, "Any luck yet on her reaching out to you?"

I shat myself when I heard that. I thought the barista was asking if I had reached out to Megan, but she responded with "Nope not yet. I sent in the book yesterday but, fingers crossed, I'll find out by the end of the week."

The Barista replied, "Well, best of luck and let me know as soon as you hear. I'm so excited for you two." Megan and Sarah

---

5   *Sveekaar* = acceptance (Hindi)

left the coffee shop without noticing me.

I would have thought seeing them would have enraged me, but it didn't. Both Ashley and Sveekaar asked me if I had ever seen my mum *that happy* before. The shocking thing was, I hadn't. Then again, how the hell was I supposed to remember, she stopped living with us when I was eleven.

Ashley asked, "Was the other half of the necklace the part that your mum gave you?" This caused a flood of unexpected emotions to rush through my body. Sveekaar got up and hugged me asking, "When was the last time you saw your mum?"

"Not since my sixteenth birthday when I told her to stop seeing me."

It was time to leave, and as we got up, slowly grazing my hand, Ashley made her way in for a hug. I didn't really think anything of it, but it was unexpected.

Sveekaar said, "I know this isn't my place, and this is a hard thing to do, but if my mum were that happy, maybe it shows that everything happens for a reason. You're just not sure what you have to learn from your parents' divorce yet." On that note, Sveekaar left, but Ashley stayed back a minute.

"Kaiya, if you ever need to talk, just call me," she said, before grabbing my phone and putting in her number. I just nodded in acknowledgement. Ashley went in for one final hug and gave me a kiss on my right cheek. Immediately I pushed her away, keeping my voice down as to not make a scene.

"What are you doing? I'm not into girls like that," Ashley looked taken aback and apologised.

"I don't normally misjudge situations like this, but you clearly still need time…"

I exclaimed as I stormed out of the cafe, "I don't need time, I don't like girls!" *Wait, did I just like that? I think I did. Kaiya, shut up. No, you did not. Girls are bad, remember what Megan did and she liked girls…* I was conflicted. The nagging thoughts, the voice, the nutcase or as I liked to call her "the crackhead" wouldn't stop rambling. I had never felt such a rollercoaster of emotions before in such a short space of time.

Dad Knows Best

Have you ever had one of those days when everything was fine but all you wanted to do was put on your favourite playlist, have an endless amount of country road and just drive?

These drives usually ended with a tub of cookie dough ice cream and watching *The Hundred-Foot Journey*. Fortunately, what I thought was going to be a day of complete desolation turned into one of total revelation. What Asveekaar had said to me about same-sex marriages and boys being shorter than you had made me highly pensive but also full of doubt. After seeing me scoff down an entire tub of ice cream and cocooned within a pyramid of pillows and blankets, my dad and I had one of the best conversations ever.

I had always blamed Megan for everything that had gone wrong, but my dad brought my behaviour towards him, compared with her to my attention. He reminded me that I never used to yell at him and blame him for anything and how I always took his side. I always thought that she had hurt him, that's why after so many years I had never seen him date another woman. He had forgiven my mother, and they were actually really good friends. Even to this day, I use this as a benchmark to remind myself that if someone can break your heart and you can find the strength to forgive them, you'll be able to get through most things in life.

Dad pulled me out of my fortress of solitude, and we spoke about several things that day, but a couple of things stood out. First was, "I need you to know that it doesn't matter whether you love a boy or a girl. I don't care, I never will care. All I care about is that they treat you right, they're a good person and make you happy." This was such a relief because I had always fought the part of myself that knew it liked girls. I always felt conflicted but when he said that to me it was like yin and yang merged into one and I was no longer split in two. We were not a religious family by any means, somewhat spiritual, but I had always had this fear of disappointing my dad by liking girls, especially as he was from an Asian background.

He taught me that height, race, gender, all of it doesn't mean anything when you click with the right person but thinking it does would affect my future (and all of humankind) going forward. He called it a "limiting belief." Two close family friends who I call Uncle James and Uncle Saint epitomise this as James has been with his husband for over eighteen years and has two children. While Saint, who is only five-foot-four, has been married to a stunning five-foot-seven Latina for over twenty-five years and they met back in school.

Secondly, my dad taught me something that my Dadu[6] had taught him when he was growing up, and that was "When you reach your lowest point that is when you are open to the greatest change." I never looked at low points like that before; it was eye-opening.

When I woke up in the morning, the tennis ball in my throat had reduced dramatically. I felt light, elated, high, ready for the day. I was happy for the first time waking up, and I began to realise what I wanted. Over the coming months, before I started university, I stopped hanging out with Ikari, Fuan, Hihan, and Asveekaar and spent more time with Rio, Ashley, and Sveekaar. I received my A-level results and managed to get into Bath University, while Ashley got into Bristol so it meant we would be close to one another. I didn't feel like there were two Kaiya's anymore, the scared bisexual and the overpowering nasty pain addict. It really felt like the unkind part of me was disappearing as I spent more time with Sveekaar, Rio and Ashley, while the scared bisexual started to turn into someone far more confident but also more loving.

Sitting under my favourite willow tree looking across the school grounds, Ashley and I soaked in the memories we had created during the last few months together. It was also nice to hear the many different types of laughs and the usual lunchtime shenanigans that occurred for one final time. I was really going

---

6   Dadu is what I called my paternal grandad because I couldn't say Dada as a kid. Anyway, the name stuck as my cousins also call their grandad Dadu too.

to miss this place. The two of us had grown close, and I was feeling more self-assured and self-confident.

"Ashley, I know that you're into girls and I've always said that I don't like them like that, but I realised I did, and I still do. I knew this from when I was about fourteen when I first saw you because I had instant butterflies. I'm sorry for the way I acted that day in the café. Also… I like you too."

"I knew you just needed time!" Ashley said, laughing. From that moment on, I embraced liking both boys and girls.

RIO

Ménage-a-Trois

As a little yout,[7] I loved food (who doesn't) but let's just say I loved it a little too much. The smell of a sizzling tandoori platter, freshly baked pizza with so much mozzarella that it would fall off en route to your mouth and, of course, the *piece de resistance*, warm chocolate-chip cookies with cookies-and-cream gelato. Food would lie next to me at night with one eye open, always watching, waiting patiently in the shadows to deliver its next hunger pang and make my mouth salivate. Inspiring my dreams with pools of mint chutney and clouds of fluffy garlic naan.

This love affair would affect my self-confidence until I was given a gym membership for my sixteenth birthday. Even with this new release, one thing remained consistent: the nagging thoughts, the voice, the nutcase or as I liked to call him "the crackhead", still wouldn't shut up. I had two prevailing thoughts which seemed to be the root of everything. This dance between me and these emotions would be a ménage-a-trois that lasted for many years. My height and weight issues were gasoline on fire for the crackhead. This gasoline, in turn, gave birth to a new source of fuel, one that would be a renewable source of energy, a never-ending supply for my crackhead to feast on. This desire was to be a Titan of industry. Watching video after video of the greatest humans alive – Tiger Woods, Michael Jordan, Steve Jobs, Bill Gates and Iron Man – all led me to develop a mindset of wanting excellence all the time from a young age. Yet even with this type of thinking, I still always felt like I was a walking basketball.

I was the youngest sibling of two older brothers and an older sister. One of my brothers, Miguel, was a hotshot property developer while the other, Jaz, was a successful

---

7   Young person

personal trainer. My sister, Carla, was a teacher, so I never felt like I was competing with her, but I was the shortest out of the three brothers. Both were stronger, in shape and successful, so I naturally felt in competition with them. They used to tease me all the time, which only fuelled the cycle of self-hate, pity, anger, motivation and self-doubt on repeat. Even so, I was still determined to always try and improve.

As you can probably tell my self-esteem was quite low, so when it came to female attention, I always felt like I was lacking. Nevertheless, there was this girl at school, Maya, who I was determined to ask out before the Easter Ball. A descendent of Italian and Turkish parents, with caramel skin and sapphire blue eyes, she had the personality of someone eight-foot-tall (thankfully she was only five-foot-two).

Losing weight definitely helped my all-round confidence, but it was still hugely lacking. I needed to be a Tiger Woods, a Bill Gates, a Titan and looking back it's no coincidence that the two places I felt most confident and calm were DT and on the golf course. Being at my local golf club always helped me feel closer to Tiger Woods. Monday nights during the summer would consist of watching the sunset on an evergreen landscape, hearing the sound of golf balls being rifled with the odd shout of "fore" and drinking an ice-cold bottle of Coca-Cola. It always helped me get away from the family, from school and from any other life issues.

I was at school; it was a Thursday afternoon, and I was working in DT on a project with Kaiya. I thought she was attractive but little things like the fact she had to be the one to grab the saws of the top shelf because I couldn't reach them, really pissed me right off. I didn't like that feeling. I felt fully emasculated. As a guy, I felt I shouldn't have to rely on a woman for help.

"Doug, I'm surprised you're able to even reach the desk, let alone fit into adult clothes. I've never seen someone at your age not actually grow," said Urami.[8]

---

8   *Urami* = resentment (Japanese)

This lovely individual you've just met, Urami, was one of two problems I had at school, and it just so happened they were in my DT class. The second problem was never far away, and I believe he is about to make his entry now.

"Leave him alone, he literally gets on with his work and does nothing to bother you. Why do you always have to be such an ass?" I intervened.

Dar[9] (whose real name was Edgar) interjected, "Looks like we have struck the same old nerve with Rio."

There you go, this was my second problem. Urami and Dar amplified my crackhead like there was no tomorrow. They were as infuriating as my siblings, but I couldn't hit them.

"You haven't struck any nerve at all. I'm just telling you to stop picking on him like you do every session."

"Rio, we will do what we want when we want. Anyway, it's not like you could do anything about it even if we didn't stop," said Urami as she looked down at me.

"Honestly, I'm surprised that Kaiya even wants to work with someone like you. Always so angry and defensive about everything. Besides, everybody knows the school preferred your older siblings. Why can't you be more like them?" said Dar.

I didn't like them picking on Doug. It always struck a nerve with me. Even when they were talking to him, I felt like they were talking to me. Doug just remained quiet and ignored the comments, but I couldn't. I took those words that Urami had said personally. Kaiya just stood their quietly as I became silent and my face turned red.

Don't worry, Rio, we know how ambitious you are. Your drive is higher than anyone I know. Don't listen to them. You're going to do amazing things in this life, stuff they couldn't even dream about. Forget them, and let's get on with work. Use this to fuel that fire in you. Forget them. My crackhead had calmed me down. Reminding myself of where I was going to end up always helped centre me and remind me of the bigger picture. Anyone could get absorbed

---

9   *Dar* = fear (Hindi)

into the present, and I hated being like anyone else. Conforming to the norm would leave me with a never-ending itch.

I continued to work as I always did now that I was feeling better. "Kaiya, we need to finish putting the whole project together before the deadline on Monday."

"Sorry, Rio, I have to go now as I have plans after school. Let's try and meet tomorrow during the day to finish. I spoke to Mr Barnes, and he said we can't come in on Saturday, so it has to be done tomorrow."

"Don't worry, we'll finish it on time."

Kaiya was the last to leave, allowing Saint and me to work alone. Saint was my best friend. He was an inch or so taller than me, but built, confident and always had a smile on his face. It was something I aspired to have one day.

"Watch Saint, I'm going to finish the project tonight and surprise her when she comes in tomorrow to see it."

"Go on then. I'm looking forward to seeing what you produce" replied Saint.

I spent the entire night working on the project (okay I got kicked out at 8 pm by the cleaning staff), but the next day as we walked into DT our project was waiting there in the middle of the room. We had decided to build a portable DJ table that changed and lit up with music. I made sure to arrive early so that I could do the classic ringmaster reveal. The "wow" moment was mine. Kaiya and Saint entered the room to see a myriad of flashing lights playing Ed Sheeran's "Don't."

"Jesus Christ, I didn't expect you to actually finish it. Rio this is actually amazing, I knew you were good at this, but the amount of passion you put into our project is on another level," Kaiya said.

"GHEEEEEEEEEEEEEZ *(in the high-pitched tone of a prepubescent choir boy)*. SOOOOOORRY SOOOOOOORY. Wow, you get the edges so smooth, you must have been sanding for hours?" Saint said excitedly.

"Wow, Rio. That's really impressive." Elissia was another girl in class who always got high grades, so a compliment from her meant a lot.

"Well, you know me, if you're going to do something, do it right or as I like to say if you're going to go in, go balls deep or don't go at all."

"Ahahahah, 100 per cent," Saint said as he fist-bumped me.

"Erghhh, Rio, you always know how to ruin it, don't you," said Kaiya rolling her eyes while laughing at me. "Thanks for getting this done. Genuinely, it is actually amazing." The combination of satisfaction from the comments I'd just received put me on an emotional high.

I decided to use this confidence to ask Maya out. Lunchtime approached, and I made my way over to her as everyone else headed out into the courtyard. My heart was pumping, but I also felt calm. I loved the adrenaline rush and being able to execute when under pressure like this. I figured this was the type of rush the Titans experienced and I wanted to get comfortable with that sort of feeling from an early age.

"Wagwan, Maya, what are you doing this Saturday?"

"Haha, hey Rio, umm, I'm not too sure. Probably something with the girls as usual."

"Well, I thought maybe we could go for dinner and bowling on Saturday evening… Make it a date." My heart was pumping. I felt like I was in a state of flow. I didn't think. My nerves were accelerating, but the adrenaline was awesome.

"Sorry, Rio, you're not actually my type." The crackhead was set off. *GHADHERO*[10] *Don't worry, Rio, let's dive deeper, find out why.*

"Let me guess, your type is Blake then?" Blake was the captain of the rugby team, confident, and his physique was similar to that of a Greek god.

"Actually, he's not really. I see why people find him good looking, but he isn't my type either."

"So, what is your type then if Blake or I don't match?"

"I like Idris' type. You know quietly confident, doesn't really care about what other people think of him. I like someone also a bit taller than me too, like Doug."

---

10 *Ghadhero* = Donkey (Gujarati)

"Wait Doug is shorter than me!" *Is this bird crazy? WTF is going on here. Forget this. I knew this wasn't a good idea. Sort yourself out, Rio, you need to start earning some money. Then girls will like you.*

"Is he? I guess I had never really noticed. He always makes me laugh anyway, so I like being around him."

"Seriously so it's because I'm too short then? I can't help that." *Really…*

"I don't think it's because you're too short, but you're always obsessing about your height and having to prove yourself. Doug and Idris don't act like that. I need to meet my friends. Sorry, Rio." The feeling of rejection kicked me right in the gut. My back felt like the sun had been beating down on it for hours.

"Okay, no worries, Maya, catch you later," I said as she walked away. That was the first time someone had addressed my height insecurity to my face. I left school that day feeling confused. I had always thought that my height was the issue, but after hearing what Maya had said, I didn't know what to believe.

Average Height of a Girl

Maya's words had rocked me to my core, but my crackhead wouldn't allow me to believe it. I just kept getting bombarded with thoughts of needing to earn money, be in better shape, have a vision for the future and for success. I didn't tell anybody about asking Maya out, but I knew it would eventually get around the year because at school gossip spread like chlamydia in a brothel.

Saint eventually questioned me about it. "Rio, why didn't you tell me?" He said angrily as we sat on a bench overlooking the edge of the quad,[2]

"Why do you think? She obviously said no," I responded with a face like a slapped ass.

"Did you bring up the height thing? I told you we can't change that."

"No, she said it wasn't because I wasn't tall enough, but didn't like that I always have to try and prove myself. She said she liked Doug."

"Wait, seriously, he's short though?"

"Yeah, she said he always makes her laugh, and she's never noticed his height."

"See! I told you. It is how you carry yourself," Saint said as he sat up straighter and with a good posture.

"If I was my brother's height, I know I'd have been fine with it, and she would have said yes." *You're getting angry aren't you Rio. Use this as fuel. Go train, focus, work, do something. To be in the 1 per cent, you need to harness this type of fuel. How many people can get pissed off like this and actually use it for work? Nobody in this school can. Time to go.*

I left Saint and headed to the library at school. I worked on my Business A-level, learning the ins and outs of how to create an IPO (initial public offering). I knew my company was going to be big one day and to be one of those Titans, best to know how to do this from a young age. My Business A-level enhanced my entrepreneurial savvy while DT inspired my innovative lust.

Sveekaar was one of my close mates at school too. His twin Asveekaar was a good-looking girl, but a right bitch. Thankfully he was pretty chilled out, a lover of both Shakespeare and English literature while also an engineering enthusiast. He and I were walking to class when we bumped into Kaiya.

"Kaiya, anything with your mum yet?" said Sveekaar.

"No, not yet, but I tell you what I've been feeling a lot better since I've not seen your sister and the rest of the girls for a while."

"Is everything okay with your mum?" I was concerned.

"Yeah, don't worry about it."

At that moment, Urami and Dar walked past the group.

"Dar how weird would it be to see Kaiya and Rio as a couple?"

It wouldn't be that weird. Rio, it's fine, your girlfriend when you leave university will be an 11 out of 10. People will snap their necks, turning to get a look at her when she walks into a room, and she will be yours, my crackhead piped up.

"I couldn't agree more Urami. It would look so peculiar, wouldn't it."

It felt like the temperature had just rose. I decided to maintain my silence as frankly I couldn't be bothered with their shit today.

"Don't worry Rio, I've realised it doesn't matter how tall or short you are. If you two, make one another happy, then that's all that matters. Anyway, I need to get to class now, I'll see you later." *Well, that was weird, she is the second person to tell me my height doesn't mean anything. Maybe it doesn't? YES, it does Rio! That is your driver for your success.* Kaiya ran off to class and Sveekaar, and I made our way to private study. We sat down and began working.

"Oi, Sveekaar," I tried to whisper across the class. But he ignored me.

"Ghadhero," I whispered again. Nobody knew what that meant at school so always got away with it.

"What do you want? I'm trying to work," said Sveekaar as he lifted his head from his books. I gestured for him to come and sit next to me so I could speak to him. He knew if he did, he wouldn't get any work done, but as a good mate does, he sacked his work off.

"Okay, what?" Sveekaar said as he sat down next to me.

"If you were a girl, you wouldn't think I was too short right?" Sveekaar looked at me with a face that said: "What in the hell did you just ask me?" Before responding with, "Da fuq?!"[11]

"Look I know I'm too short for a lot of girls, but I never expected the girls who are shorter than me to say I'm too short as well."

"You're a right crackhead. What do you want me to say?" Sveekaar sounded bewildered.

"Tell me I'm right."

"Well, you're wrong then. And it is your fault you are like this."

"Are you joking? I didn't ask for this, and yet I have to deal with it all. Why am I asking you? You're five foot ten. It doesn't matter to you." Sveekaar rolled his eyes into the back of his head as he had heard this before.

"It is not your fault that you are short. You are right; you had no choice in that. It is your fault for letting it affect you so much."

"No, it's not. If I was taller, I wouldn't feel like this. Like my brother. He's five-foot-seven and doesn't have any of these issues."

"If you were five-foot-seven, you would complain you weren't five-foot-ten. People who are five-foot-ten complain they're not six-foot. This wouldn't change."

"I guess I'd never thought of that. But life would be so much easier. You would be less likely to be rejected. I've heard the average height of the most successful people is around five-foot-seven, five-foot-eight."

"Rio, let me ask you this. If you were given a box of shit, and you knew it was a box of shit, would you accept it or discard it?" *WTF kind of a stupid question is this. Rio just go with it, you never know what you may learn.*

---

11 Da fuq = What the fuck?

"I'd bake a cake with it. What do you think, I wouldn't put my hands anywhere near it."

"So, when Urami and Dar make comments about your height, why do you accept it and let it get to you. You're essentially holding onto the box of shit, and you're upset that you're holding this box of shit. Yet you are the one who said yes to keeping it." Sveekaar slightly raised his voice as he tended to when he made a point. "Why are you accepting their box of shit?"

Shit, I never ever thought of this like this. This guy has mind fucked me. The bell rang for the end of the day, and the two of us began packing up. I was lost in my own thoughts after that.

"Rio, just because you see your insecurity, doesn't mean other people do, remember that" said Sveekaar.

I wasn't sure what to say in reply, but I went to bed that night with a million thoughts racing through my head.

Finding Easter Eggs

I began questioning, maybe my height isn't the be-all and end-all. I had been going back and forth with this in my head, and the crackhead helped me reframe my thoughts. I began thinking: *My height may not matter, but I'm now going to prove that to be successful, it doesn't matter about your height. In fact, if I can do it, anyone can do it. No excuses."*

Redefining my crackhead with this new outlook helped me slowly overcome this feeling I had in the bottom of my stomach. It's funny how things work because I started thinking differently about my height, life reminded me that I didn't have a date for the Easter Ball. It was tonight. Brilliant! I was eighteen, I was going to university in six months, I hadn't been close to having a girlfriend, let alone having sex. I had my first kiss when I was seventeen (okay, technically I had my first kiss when I was seven when the boys and girls played kiss chase in the playground.) I had seen all of these US TV shows about losing your virginity at a ball or prom, and this was essentially the equivalent for us. *American Pie* really didn't set any good expectations for me. It didn't help that Saint used to call me *Shitbrick* at times. Also, as I couldn't play an instrument, I was not allowed to go to band camp. I went to the dance with Saint and Sveekaar, and we met Kaiya and Ashley there. I felt good being dressed in all black. I had to have the best suit and smell the nicest, but I couldn't look like everyone else. I needed to be different, so I wore a bowtie. Yes, that was my fashion statement for the evening. My confidence had taken a real knock, and I felt like that chubby thirteen-year-old again.

I was pensive, so I just sat there for most of the night on a table while everyone was up and dancing. I wasn't feeling in the party spirit, but when I realised being a miserable little bitch is what anyone else would do in this situation, I decided to prove a point to myself to go and have fun.

Oi, you can't be like everyone else. This is what 99 per cent of the population does. The 1 per cent don't let a girl stop them.

Yes, they do. Even the 1 per cent have their confidence knocked.

My crackhead was tormenting me, playing on both sides of the argument but then I remembered what Sveekaar had said and headed to the dancefloor to enjoy myself with my friends.

After that, we did shots, we danced, and whenever I was on the dancefloor (not professionally, just club music), I didn't let anything faze me. Laughing with my friends, enjoying music and making the most of the night, I began to enjoy myself. Sveekaar was right, nobody else saw my insecurity until I kept pointing it out and this applied to confidence too. I was at least going to try and fake it until I made it. After dancing for a while, I sat back down at the table to grab a drink when Elissia approached me.

"Hey Rio, I loved the work you did in DT. Your project was so cool."

"Thanks, Elissia. Yeah, Kaiya and I worked really hard on it."

Damn, she looks good. Rio, you should compliment her, came crackhead's voice.

NO, don't do that! Just chill out.

"I know Kaiya helped you, but I saw the amount of passion you put into your work and I really admire that."

"Really?"

"Yeah, I think it's really attractive when someone is passionate about something."

Da fuq? Is she flirting with me? Rio, she is flirting with you! I repeat she is flirting. At this point, Saint and Sveekaar make eye contact with me. Saint pretended to bend Sveekaar over on the dancefloor and smack his ass like any typical degenerate teenage boy boosting their friend's confidence in the quest to hook-up with a female.

"Well, darlin' like I always say, if you're going to do something, go balls… I mean to do it right." Why the fuck did I just go cockney? I am a right plonker. Thank God you didn't say go balls deep in front of her.

"You were about to say go balls deep, weren't you?" she said laughing.

My eyes shot out of my head. OH SHIT. How da fuq did she know that?!

"Errrr…"

"Don't worry, I've heard you say it before and found it funny."

Rio, compliment this girl now! NO, Shut up. Just keep the conversation going.

"Well you're the first girl I know to find that funny," I said, shocked I managed to respond.

"Rio, I'm going to be upfront, how come you've never asked me out?"

"HUH?!" I nearly choked on my drink. "Wait, what? Seriously?"

"Seriously. I've seen you staring at me before," she said, sipping her drink.

"Err…" Oh shit… what do I say?

"Haha, don't worry I was staring too, and we've always got along well."

Is this a dream, like who the hell has this level of confidence at eighteen? Rio, you need to learn from her. She would be good for you. COMPLIMENT HER NOW!

"Well, I thought I was too short for you, so I didn't bother initially, but now I've actually begun to realise that my height matters only if I let it. Also, I think you're really attractive too." Go on, Rio. Well done. Finally, your balls have dropped. Well done you now have a pair of Easter eggs.

"Aww, that's sweet. Rio, you're funny and passionate. Honestly, you need to give yourself some more credit."

"I've never met anyone as direct as you before, El. Do you mind if I call you El?" Rio! Why are you making up nicknames? Don't do that – you absolute idiot.

"No, I quite like that. Why don't we go and dance?"

Oh shit, she liked it. I was so confused. I couldn't believe this was happening. "Let's go."

The two of us danced for the rest of the night. I noticed Kaiya staring at me on a few occasions but wasn't sure what to make of it. For once, I decided not to overthink and enjoy the moment. I figured if something was meant to be it will be.

***

Two months had passed, and Elissia and I had begun dating. My confidence was high, and I felt good about myself. I had been spending more time with El, and the two of us were headed for Bath University to study Design and Engineering. I also stopped listening to Urami and Dar's continuous petty rubbish too. They could say what they wanted, but I decided not to accept their box of shit anymore. Enough was enough. I don't like being like anybody else, and I realised that by reacting to their comments, I was like everyone else. If I let it go and looked at all the good in my life, I knew I would stand out (at least in my own head I thought so).

El and I were enjoying our final day of school, June 21, 2015. "I honestly cannot believe that I have a girlfriend now and that she is taller than me. Four months ago, I wouldn't have even allowed myself to think of a situation like this."

"Oh, really?"

"Yeah, it's so funny how things align when you become content within yourself."

"Well, you know I don't care about those types of things, but I'm glad it doesn't bother you either anymore. Plus, I'm only like four inches taller, and you make me feel like I'm a model."

"Oh shit, I never thought of that." See Rio, this girl is good for you. She is making you change your entire perspective on things already. I felt something changing in me, a calm that I had never felt before and a release in my anger. This was something that I was thrilled about and couldn't wait to see how it progressed now that I had let go of this old belief system.

Swadhisthana
(Sacral Chakra)

WATER

Kaiya: "Everything happens for a reason."[12]

*Rio: "This lone gunslinger act is unnecessary...
you don't have to do this alone."*[13]

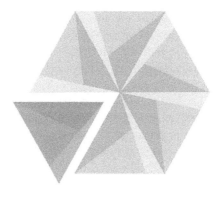

---

12 Ninety per cent of the global population

13 *Iron Man II* (2010). Marvel Studios

The Joys of University...

The summer after school had finished was one of the best. I was in love with someone for the first time, although I never imagined it to be a girl. Dad loved meeting her, and Ashley and I were inseparable. We even took a small holiday together to Paris, where we spent our three-month anniversary. It was Dad's idea as he wanted to make sure I got the most out of every moment with her. He always used to remind me to enjoy the moments while they lasted, because once they were gone, that would be it.

Today was a huge day for me – moving-in day. I felt like I had made progress in forgiving Megan as the anger and rejection I used to feel had reduced dramatically, but I still wasn't ready to see her just yet. Ashley tried to convince me to meet up with her before this new chapter began. It wasn't easy because I felt anxious every time I thought about seeing her.

Dad and I pulled up to the halls of residence, and there was a sea of students and parents all from different backgrounds. I had never lived around boys like this before, so I was quite nervous. Rio and Sveekaar were always so easy to get on with at school, but Dad always reminded me that things would take a bit of time to settle down. Of course, this information went in one ear and out the other.

There were seven of us in my flat: three boys and four girls, including me. Of the boys, one was adopted, and one had lived in eight different countries. The third lad was twenty-two and a dad to a five-year-old girl. Of us girls, I noticed Alisha in particular. She was a similar height to me, a powerlifter and was also studying English. Her eyes were so seductive, every time I looked at them, I wanted to get naked. Her accent was an aphrodisiac, a mixture of African and South American. It sent tingles down my back. This was the first time I had felt such strong emotions like this since meeting Ashley, but I knew that was okay. At the end of the day as long as I never acted upon it, there was nothing wrong with admiring someone else's beauty.

As the term went on, I became friends with Maaphee[14] (the twenty-two-year-old dad with a kid), but Alisha and I became especially close. Nothing was happening, but I felt like it would have been the Fourth of July, Christmas and Diwali all intertwined if it did.

It wasn't until partway into the term though that I realised university was not the "best time of your life" as every adult had ever told me before. Deadlines, exams and essays were not a part of my "formula" for fun. It was supposed to be drinking, eating, sex and general debauchery. (Not necessarily with different people, but I genuinely thought I would be engaging in nooky a few times a week – how wrong I was.)

The stress of work began to hit me hard, and that's when I met Suto. Suto was in my English class and at first, seemed nice, but always made remarks like, "I know we only had to read these five books, but I've tried to read at least twelve" or "Oh, you've only got these many references, I think maybe you should be doing a bit more work than socialising. I've already got my summer internship sorted for the end of the first year."

I tried to not let her remarks affect me as I knew she was tactical – she wanted to be top of the class. Part of me took it as a compliment because it meant that she felt threatened by me, but at the same time, her words penetrated the back of my head like a bullet from a rifle. After freshers' week had ended, which involved a plethora of drinking and conversations starting with "We're going to have so much fun over the next three years…" while knocking back a Jägerbomb, I decided to head to Bristol.

It was sometime in October 2015 when I surprised Ashley. I was stressed out with work, Suto had really been getting to me, and I thought a bit of TLC with my "friend" (not quite

---

14 Maaphee = forgiveness (Hindi)

sure what you want to call it as we never put a label on it) would do me some good. She and I had spoken twice a week religiously, but we tried to make an effort not to get stuck with the idea of only having one another and not making any other friends. I got to Bristol, and as I walked into her hall to surprise her, I found her on the bed lying in some other girl's lap.

"What in God's name is going on here!"

"Oh my God, Kaiya, we were just talking about you. Wait, did we plan to meet today?" She looked confused.

"No, I thought I would surprise you and make dinner." My sarcastic undertone was overwhelmed with anger and jealously.

"I was telling Kelsey how much I missed you and that I wanted to see you."

"Well, you look like you didn't miss me *that* much." At that point, Kelsey got up off the bed and introduced herself to me. "I'll give you two some time."

"Thanks, Kelsey, I'll see you later," said Ashley. I remember looking at Kelsey's big brown eyes. They were like pools of golden honey. That was something Ashley said she loved about me. Something felt wrong, but I thought, I needed to give her the chance to explain.

"It was nice to meet you, Kaiya. You really are as stunning as Ashley said," Kelsey said, before leaving the two of us together.

"Before you get angry, because I know what you're like as soon as you see red, Kelsey has a boyfriend. They've been together for a year; you have nothing to be worried about." At this point, I did calm down, but I didn't know what to believe. The thought of the two of them together just made me associate some form of feeling with Megan. It felt like that rejection had come back, but I knew I had to control it because she was allowed to have other female friends, and I had to trust her. I took a few deep breaths and calmed down.

Ashley and I spent the rest of the weekend, eating, drinking and shagging. I didn't think at all about Alisha until I got back to Bath – it was actually a bit of relief knowing that. This is what university life was about. We were lying together basking in the afterglow smoking a joint and enjoying The Weeknd's *Beauty Behind the Madness* album. It was everything I had thought university would be, but I couldn't get that crackhead at the back of my brain to shut up. I knew Kelsey was only a few doors away, and Suto had really got to me about the volume of work she had done, so I left early Monday morning as I became more and more anxious. I had this sickly feeling of leaving Ashley here with Kelsey but remembering that I had Alisha back at Bath comforted me. Ashley was loyal and trusting, and I knew she would trust me to be friends with Alisha as it would show more about my character, so I decided to do the same, reluctantly.

A few weeks went by, and Ashley and I became more distant. She started avoiding my calls or being too busy to chat and text. If we spoke, we ended up having a dispute and more often than not, it was about Kelsey. This all happened within the first eight weeks of university, so by this point in time, I was missing my dad a lot. It had been the longest period I had been away from him, so I was so excited to go back home and see him.

Rahul

Every Friday evening during the summer, Dad and I would have chilli paneer and chicken wings outside in our garden while enjoying a glass of Shiraz. I enjoyed the dry texture of the wine accompanied by the myriad of spices coating the chicken and paneer. I would never forget this time I spent with him as our nights usually ended with a hidden story from his past that I'd never heard before.

On my journey home I bumped into Rio on the train. He seemed different: calm, smiling and full of joy – something I only ever saw in him when he was working in DT at school. We caught up with each other's events from the last eight weeks, but every time he mentioned Elissia, I felt a bit of a kick in my gut. I couldn't understand why. Rio was my friend, but the night of Easter ball when he and Elissia were dancing, I had never seen him so at ease and happy. Did I fancy Rio? I wasn't sure. The fact I was having issues with Ashley only fuelled my crackhead. Part of me wished I made him feel like that, but how could I expect him to like me when I'd been such an awful person for a long time at school. Next thing I knew, it was my turn to share.

"How are things with you and Ashley?" Rio asked.

"They're alright, we've both been working so we haven't seen one another that much recently but we're all good." Why am I lying to him? *You have been friends since school. You don't need to lie to him Kaiya. Just tell him, it may help you feel better. Actually, on second thought you will feel better once you are home.* Thankfully the train got into Euston and as Rio and as I departed, I called my dad.

"Hey, Dad, do you want me to bring home dinner?"

"Hello darling, I don't mind, we could go out for food."

"Let's have our usual Friday night. Open a bottle of Shiraz please."

"Okay, sweetie, love you and see you when you are home."

"Love you too, Dad, see you shortly."

***

I picked up the food and made my way home. "Dad, where are you? I bought our favourite – the wings and chilli paneer." I wasn't sure where he was. I went straight to the kitchen to serve the food, but he still hadn't come in to say hi to me. This was a bit odd now. Where could he be? When I walked into the living room, I couldn't believe what I saw.

"Dad, what on earth are you doing?" He was on the floor bent over, looking for something under the sofa, but he didn't respond. I tapped him on the head, but he didn't move. "Dad? What are you doing?" He used to like playing jokes on me, and I couldn't tell if this was one of them, so I pushed him onto his side, but he wasn't moving.

"Dad, wake up," I yelled. I shook his body. I slapped his face. He wasn't breathing. I dialled 999 for an ambulance, and they told me to start CPR. I was pressing down on his chest for what felt like an eternity before the paramedics arrived to take over. That tennis ball feeling was back, and I had succumbed to every fearful thought imaginable. They performed their procedures trying to get him to wake up, but nothing was working. They ripped his shirt open.

"Three, two, one… Clear," said one of the paramedics.

"Clear," responded the other.

Dad's body moved up and down, but nothing. They repeated this, again and again, increasing the voltage each time. I'll never forget that sinking feeling when one of the paramedics said, "Time of death 18:42."

I ran straight to the toilet to be sick

I wanted the ground to open up and swallow me whole. I didn't want to be in a world without my dad. I didn't know what to do. The paramedics loaded his body into the ambulance. I called Ashley five times, but they all went to voicemail so I called Rio and he answered.

"Rio, Rio, Rio, my dad's just di–" Rio couldn't understand what I was saying as I physically couldn't say the words.

I passed the phone to one of the paramedics, mumbling "Tell him." I could hear Rio yelling on the phone, "Kaiya, hello."

"Okay, Kaiya. Hello Rio."

"Hello, who is this?"

"This is the paramedic, and I'm at Kaiya's house. Regrettably, her dad has just passed away. It looks like it was a heart attack."

"What the hell! Tell her I'm on my way right now."

"Okay, I'll let her know."

The paramedics waited with me until Rio and his family got there. A fun evening of food and catching up with my dad turned into a boxing match with life where it had just thrown the biggest body blow, I could have ever imagined. Never before had I felt so alone. Rio's parents invited me to stay with them for as long as I needed to. That same day I had to call Megan, but I couldn't do it. I didn't know what to say or how to say it. Rio grabbed the phone out of my hand and did it for me.

"Hello? Is this Megan?"

"Sorry, who is this?"

"This is Rio, I'm a friend of Kaiya's. I'm at her house now with my family."

"Is everything alright? What's going on?"

"You're going to need to sit down. Rahul seems… he had a heart attack and passed away."

As he said that I grabbed the phone from him.

"Mum, it's Kaiya. Dad's gone. He is really gone." I was crying into the phone. The tears couldn't come out quick enough. The salty tinge dripped into my mouth. I had been rocked to my core. I didn't know what to expect. My dad has just died, and my mum was on route to the house. This was going to be the first conversation we'd had in years.

Thankfully, I was able to speak to Alisha before Megan got there, and she told me, "Just forget about the past for tonight and to just be with your mum."

***

When the doorbell rang, it reverberated through my chest and sent my body into another state of shock. I felt as though I'd be sick again.

Rio opened the door, and as soon as Megan stepped into the living room, every single thought imaginable actually left my head. All I heard was "Go hug her", and I sobbed into her chest. Sarah was with her, but I didn't acknowledge her. This was the first time I had met her, but I knew it wasn't going to be the last. The rest of the night was a blur, Megan and I didn't actually speak much, but I just lay on her lap crying until I fell asleep.

Rio woke me up when he was leaving with his family, and I left with them. As I was leaving, Megan told me to stay with her, but after looking at her and Sarah, I still couldn't do it. I thought I had really moved passed this, but it felt like every possible form of pain had hit me at once.

The crackhead was surprisingly quiet for an occasion of this magnitude, and that was the only bit of solace I was able to take from that night. I stayed with Rio for the weekend, but we headed back to Bath for Monday lectures. I had to get out of London for the time being.

Checkmate

I knew I had a mother, but I felt like an orphan. I wasn't alone, but I felt lonely. Loneliness is a strange emotion because you can have all of the support in the world around you – every single friend looking after you as if you were royalty – and yet the only peaceful part of the day was when I had cried myself to sleep. I felt like a zombie for the next couple of weeks, that was until Ashley finally called me. I hadn't told her about Dad, but she told me she was coming to visit. This is where the fun and games really began. It was as if the crackhead was staring down at me, rubbing its hands together, getting ready to mess with me emotionally. *Maybe Rio called her and told her what happened? Maybe she is going to break up with me? Kaiya, don't stress, you don't know what is going to happen, just turn up and keep your temper under control. Just do that… Easier said than done.*

Ashley came into my bedroom and spoke for some time. Still, all I could remember afterwards was the first part of the conversation which was…" I don't think you and I are right anymore… I need to explore what university life is like… I feel caged, and the last thing I want to do is end up resenting you." Esta estupida chica.[15] Ashley had just called checkmate on our time together.

"This is about Kelsey, isn't it?"

"No, it's not! I don't know how many times I need to say this!" *Is this girl serious? You should have done more! You should have made more of an effort! Kaiya this is your fault. Actually, you don't need her. If she doesn't want to be with you, get rid of her. She is a waste of your time and energy.*

We continued arguing. I'm sure everyone in my whole flat could hear us, but I didn't care. I didn't want to tell Ashley about my dad, but then I remember hearing: *Make her feel guilty. Make her feel like shit. Make her cry. She hurt you, hurt her back.* Ashley

---

15 Meaning "This stupid girl!" in Spanish, which I started learning when I met Alisha as I wanted to converse with her.

loved my dad and always got on with him, so I knew the news would affect her too. I calmed myself down, quietened my tone and looked deep into her eyes. I wanted this to be the slow knife that she felt, not a quick gunshot to the head.

"Don't interrupt what I am about to say…" I paused for dramatic effect. "I called you that Friday evening because my dad had a heart attack. He died in the living room. You should have been there for me, and you weren't. You are one of the most selfish human beings I have ever encountered, and I never want to see you again. I'm done speaking." *Go on cry, I want you to cry. She is so close… Oh wait, there it is. Well done, Kaiya.*

I had never seen that look on Ashley's face. You would have thought her dad had just died. She sat on my bed while I just looked down on her. That feeling of hate and rejection associated with Megan had just attached itself to Ashley too. Ashley voiced her "deepest condolences and her feelings of sorrow", but I didn't want to hear them. As she left, the final words I heard from her were "I'm so sorry, Kaiya."

I was in class a few weeks later. The funeral had been and gone, and Megan kept trying to get me to stay with her over the Christmas period. I refused. I had so many exams coming up, and the combined stress and anger of everything in the last few months had become unbearable, but I didn't want to drop out of university. I had to finish for Dad at the very least. He never went and had been so proud when I got in. If I didn't do something to deal with everything that was going on, I don't know what would have happened. I was drinking a bottle of wine most days. Those few hours of numbed pain helped, but only made coming up from the depths of sorrow – to be greeted by crackhead and a thumping headache – that much harder.

I saw a leaflet for a spirituality class on the activities board in our student union one day and thought, I can't feel any worse, so I might as well try this. I remembered what Dad had told me about being at your lowest point, so I was intrigued to see.

When I arrived, the teacher asked us to sit on the floor and just start breathing. We took ten deep in-breaths and ten deep out-breaths, and then he asked us to sit peacefully. I wanted to leave within five minutes, I thought, What a load of rubbish. But as I looked over, I saw Maaphee. Maaphee had always had his head screwed on from what I knew of him, so seeing him there, made me give the class a chance. I don't know why it did, but I stayed. We did some deep breathing exercises, which made me feel like I was hyperventilating, but surprisingly the headrush was similar to smoking a menthol cigarette when you're drunk.

The teacher then asked us to focus on our thoughts. "Imagine you're flowing down a stream…" That was all I heard before I zoned out. This wasn't for me, but surprisingly my crackhead was pushing me to try it. For once, it was actually inviting me to do something for my own health. I sat there for twenty minutes of breathing, just trying not to cry. The more I tried not to think of Ashley and Dad, the more they appeared in my thoughts. I survived the full twenty minutes feeling slightly better, but excited to get a glass of wine in my hands. As I was packing my mat away, I made eye contact with Maaphee. He smiled at me and came over to give me a hug. Hugging him was like hugging the purest energy in the world. He always made me feel better with just a simple smile and hug.

"How's your head been with everything that's gone on recently?" Maaphee said as we walked back to the flat together.

"Still all over the place. I don't want to speak to Megan. I want to fight Ashley, and I'm angry at myself for letting us get into that position, and I feel so alone," I said, feeling fatigued and defeated.

"There are a lot of things going on in your life right now, and you need to realise it won't fix itself in one day. You have to give yourself time to adjust."

He sounds like Dad talking to me. This is strange…

"What do you mean?"

"Well you have told me before that you feel guilty for not trying enough with Ashley, but you can't blame yourself. You both had university to begin with. You're adjusting, and it takes two to tango. What are you angry at most?"

How on earth are words like this coming out of such a young boy's mouth? Actually, he sounds similar to Sveekaar now that I think of it.

"The fact that she wasn't there for me during all of this when I thought she would be and how I let jealousy affect me."

"Well, Ashley not being there for you is something you can't control, but your jealousy, you can. Focus on what you can control."

How the hell do you not be jealous. He is making it easier than it is. Or is it actually that easy? Wow, he's mature. Maybe I should date a boy? Should I date Maaphee? Wait, he's happily married. All I know is that women are just shit.

"Kaiya, no matter how much you think of what has happened, you'll never ever be able to change it. Start by accepting that and forgiving yourself for what's happened with her. Then begin to accept responsibility for your parts of the relationship that were bad. That's how I had to learn to get over things. Accept, forgive and move forward."

We had finally arrived back at the flat. It happened to be a Friday night, so Maaphee and I shared wings and paneer (my whole flat knew this is what I ate as I had had it every Friday night since I arrived). He shared a bottle of wine with me, and we toasted Dad. It was the first time since he died that I had felt some form of relief. A feeling of relaxation overwhelmed me. Talking to Maaphee had really helped in ways that I couldn't have imagined.

***

Over the next few months, I realised (with the help of Maaphee and these types of conversations) my jealousy was down to longing for Ashley's undivided attention – something that I had had over the summer.

Maaphee told me: "To start giving myself attention instead of expecting it from others". To some extent, I had always done stuff to please Ashley instead of doing things for myself. "Not every relationship is meant to last, but every relationship has a reason. Everything happens for a reason. What you learn from it is down to you."

I knew he was right. Things were hard as I came to slowly accept these realities, but in doing so, I became really close to Alisha. Rio and I had stayed close since the night Dad died, but whenever I saw him with El, I always backed off. I was confused with Rio and, after the last few months, I thought it would be better to focus on myself for a bit. Rio looked out for me a lot like Maaphee, but there was a different feeling here. Once I finally accepted my faults in my relationship with Ashley, she and I met up and discussed it. We accepted that we may not be friends, but I apologised for being so jealous, and how I'd behaved when she broke up with me. I'd finally found closure and forgave myself. The only piece of the puzzle that I still hadn't touched was dealing with Megan… but one step at a time.

RIO —————————————————————

Drinking, Partying and Fun... Bollox

During the first few months at university, life changed at a pace that was quicker than I expected. El and I had been dating, and it was going well. I lost my virginity to her over the summer (I wasn't her first though) and I don't think I could have finished school in a better position. I felt like I could close that chapter of my life – feeling secure: I had a stunning girlfriend and was studying a course I loved at my top choice university. El and I wondered whether it would be wise to go to uni as a couple because of everything we had heard about relationships breaking up within the first few weeks. We agreed, in the end, to continue dating, but we understood that there would be an adjustment period. She would be meeting a lot of guys, and I would be meeting a lot of girls. (Well I had hoped so at least. Watching an American TV show about university before going to a UK university was probably one of the worst ideas I had, now looking back on it. It gave me so many unrealistic expectations.)

Before I left for uni, my dad said he would help pay for my accommodation and provide me with an extra allowance to live so that I didn't need a job. In return, he wanted me to bring home a first-class degree. I always thought I was going to have to balance a job and studying, so this was probably one of the nicest things my dad had ever done for me. I was so grateful, and I was already determined to get a first anyway. Dad had to manage the family business when he was nineteen while studying. He'd had to juggle too many balls at once which meant he didn't get the full uni experience and ended up finishing with a lower second-class degree which was something he didn't want me to go through. When I told him that it would be good for me to have a job too, he simply responded, "You'll have your whole life to work, enjoy uni."

A gift of this nature which was given with pure love and nothing but good intentions somehow morphed into a target sitting on my back.

I'm telling you this because I was given a lot of shit when my course mates asked me why I didn't need a job. They said I "was given everything," or that I "didn't have to earn it the way they did," and this was something I never really expected to get from people. It made me feel worse about myself and triggered me into having the attitude of "I have to do everything for myself now."

Whenever I felt this, my crackhead would be fuelled by the commonality of the Titans. All were a part of "the struggle, the grind, the hustle" and it ended up making me resent not only my dad for a while but anyone that helped me. A year that was supposed to be filled with partying and passing exams, became one where I was determined to get high firsts in everything I did. What didn't help was that as my degree was a four-year course, and our first-year results were the deciding factor in whether we were given an industrial placement in our third year. Again, this shock to the system fuelled my resentment towards all those family friends and adults who wished to impart their words of wisdom, which usually ended with "The first year is about passing and partying, uni is the best time of your life." That turned out to be a right load of bullshit.

I missed El and wanted to spend time with her, but our schedules never seemed to line up, and it was making me feel uneasy.

One day I was sitting in my room working when there was a knock on the door, and it was her! I literally jumped at her, hugged and kissed her as if I was a little puppy excited to see their owner. Just the smell of her perfume and her conditioner aroused me and gave me such a high.

"What are you doing here?"

"Well, I thought I would surprise you as I had been missing you. Plus, you barely respond to my messages, so I wasn't sure if something was up. I thought it would be best to see you and speak to you in person."

I hadn't realised, but when I had been texting her, it wasn't the same way she was used to. I was never the biggest fan of texting, but after going through my responses to her, I realised I was coming across as blunter than usual, and that probably didn't help the situation.

"No, nothing is wrong. I'm so glad to see you," I responded.

"Well, I brought some wine and have one rule if we're going to drink it…"

"What's that?" I asked hesitantly.

"We can't leave the room until both bottles are finished, and we have to be naked as we drink it."

See! This girl is cool. This girl is sick!

After a session of what felt like raw, animalistic sex, we cuddled for hours, chatting about everything. I had never felt a high in my life like this before. I told her about what the boys had said to me and how confused I felt.

She said, "Rio, your dad is giving you such a phenomenal opportunity here. Don't waste that or think any less of it. You don't need to apologise or feel guilty because your parents have been able to do something for you that other people's have not."

She was right. I had never thought of it like that, and I wasn't going to let other people send me back into a state of flux where I felt awful about myself for something that wasn't my fault. I didn't choose to go to private school or the fact that they couldn't so I realised I mustn't let it affect me.

El stayed with me for a few days. We worked, ate, had sex and didn't leave the room. It was exactly how I thought uni was supposed to be, but then all good things have to come to an end as I was heading back to London for my first visit home since leaving the nest. I bumped into Kaiya on the train and realised we hadn't seen one another in nearly five months. For whatever reason, we didn't really hang out much over the holidays after school ended. She looked as she always did.I felt amazing after the few days I had been with El, and seeing Kaiya only reinforced how much I liked El as I no longer felt that weird feeling about Kaiya. It was nice to get this confirmation.

"How are things with you and Ashley?"

"They're alright, she is working, and so we haven't seen one another that much recently but we're all good."

I was glad things were going well for her and Ashley. Knowing that made me feel a bit more at ease. I always had fun hanging out with Kaiya at school, and ever since she stopped speaking to Ikari and the other girls, she was a lot nicer to be around.

I was at home having dinner with the family being teased about life by my brothers as usual, but for the first time, it didn't bother me. The first words they said were "Frodo's home." Before that would have triggered me and now I loved it.

Eat, Stress, Study, Repeat

The weekend I was back in London for the first time made me grow up very quickly. I got the call from Kaiya and, at first, I couldn't understand what was going on. I thought she was laughing until the paramedic came on the phone and explained. Being next to Kaiya over the next few weeks allowed me to understand a world of grief I had never imagined but one where I was essentially able to experience it without going through the loss. The issue with all of this was trying to balance being a good friend emotionally, maintain my studies and everything else uni demands.

As January approached, I began to stress about my exams. Two boys, I met on my course where Resu and Culpa. (They were bell ends of the highest order.) These were probably two people I disliked more than anyone and reminded me of Dar and Urami at school. They used to love flaunting how much work they had done. How they had revised everything. I had started going out and drinking more than I should have. I needed an escape from everything and to forget what was going on. This meant though on several occasions, I was hanging like donkey's cock (hungover) while revising and Resu and Culpa would come and remind me how far behind I was compared to them.

"You look rough Rio, out again drinking?"

"What do you want Culpa,[16] I've got work to do?" I could still feel the alcohol sitting in my stomach.

"Personally, if I were you, I would stop taking a break because it seems you just keep falling behind," said Reus.[17]

"Can you two please just leave me alone?"

"Oh yeah, Culpa, did you know I've got my internship sorted for this summer with Nike."

"That fantastic Reus, I just got news today my application to work with Google has been accepted."

---

16 *Culpa* = Guilt (Latin)
17 *Sutoreus* (Suto & Reus) = Stress (Japanese)

"Wait, you two have already got your internships sorted for this summer?" I felt so nauseous when they said that. It probably didn't help that I still had a copious amount alcohol running through my system, as it only made my anxiety worse.

"Yep, looks like you have a lot to catch up, Rio," said Reus as they both walked off. How have they got internships already? *Rio, you need to sort your shit out. Time to attack, focus on working. No more dicking around.*

I began revising twelve hours a day and applying for internships. I stopped going to the gym for about five months and began to stress eat. Every time I needed a break from work, I wanted to go out and drink, but then when I was out drinking, I felt anxious about not working, and this caused me to be even more stressed out. On top of all of this Reus and Culpa taunted me daily. The cycle was relentless.

Exam season passed, and for about a week, I just caught up on sleep. The nerves of results looming only made me stress eat even more. Finally, results day arrived. Nervous was an understatement. To top things off, I had put on weight and wasn't feeling great in my skin right now, but I thought the sacrifice would be worth it when I saw I had smashed my exams.

The grades came out, and I achieved a first in two exams, an upper second in three and a lower second in my final one. This meant my average for the first semester was an upper second (64 per cent). I had the worst sinking feeling in my stomach. *What was my dad going to say? What was wrong with me, I'd achieved 90 per cent in my A-levels, and I couldn't even get past 65 per cent here.* I knew this meant I would have to work even harder to get my average up and get a good internship – the competition was fierce. I also made a fatal error that day by checking my results online in the library. Surprise, surprise, guess who happened to be five feet away in joy about achieving the top two marks in our class.

"Don't worry Rio, I'm sure someone will hire you, and if not, there is no shame in switching courses. You just may not be built for designing," said Culpa.

"Don't listen to him, Rio," said Saint and Maaphee. Saint also got into Bath to study the same course and Maaphee and I had become friends after chatting one day in the smoker's area on a night out. He too was studying Design, a slightly different course, but we had several similar modules.

"Reus, perhaps we should leave these two to make poor old Rio feel better."

"Probably a good idea. I wouldn't want to know how he feels knowing most places won't accept him now."

Hit him. Just hit the prick in the face. No, don't do that, Rio.

The two of them left anyway leaving Maaphee, Saint and I together.

"Rio, don't worry about this, remember the long-term scope. By the end of uni, you'll have a career, money and girlfriend. You'll be smashing it," said Saint.

"Rio, just take some time to process this. Honestly, this isn't a big deal, I know you may feel like shit right now but, you've got another semester to change things so try to be a bit kind to yourself," said Maaphee as the two of them left.

I felt burnt out. I didn't want to do anything else, and at the same time, I wanted to hit the ground running for the second semester and attack all out. But I just didn't have the energy.

Hitting the Links

A few weeks passed, and I felt depressed as hell. I had lost my *joie de vivre*. Seeing El cheered me up, but it also meant as soon as she was gone, I felt even more miserable. I hadn't made it into the university golf team, but in all fairness, I threw up on the course during the day of trials as I had fresher's flu. Suffice to say I didn't play my best round of golf. I always loved being on the course, especially at sunset as it was peaceful and gave me some time to think. It always put me in a good mood, and, to quote *Happy Gilmore,* this was my "happy place."

Maaphee joined me late in the spring as the days grew longer. I didn't hit the ball well that day and, unlike other sports, if you are not calm and in control, you can't play well. I wasn't at all calm and tried to murder every drive. Finally, Maaphee got sick of looking in the trees for my ball on every hole, and we sat down on a tee box, which was the highest point and overlooked the rest of the course. It was blissfully peaceful, yet I couldn't enjoy it.

"Rio, you haven't spoken about it, but I can tell it is still on your mind, so I'm going to say it again. It's okay to not get the best grades. It doesn't define how successful you are."

What is he talking about? Yes, they are. I know he's trying to help, but he's just annoying me. "Maaphee, what are you talking about? It's very simple, good grades will mean a good job. A good job means lots of money. Lots of money means unlimited opportunities and experiences. It's black and white."

"Rio, yes money does give you several opportunities, but there is more than one way to add up to ten."

What the hell is this guy on? "What are you talking about now?"

"Okay let me clarify, you are angry at yourself for not getting a first because it means you can't earn any money?"

"Well, yes. That's the main concern."

"How many different ways can you think of to add up to the number ten?"

"Why is this relevant?"

"Just answer the question."

"Okay, five different ways."

"Only five?"

"Fine, how many can you think of?"

"Well besides the obvious, five plus five, six plus four, seven plus three, eight plus two and nine plus one, you have all the decimal values too."

"Once again, how is this relevant?"

"My point is, you think that only good grades are going to get you an internship and nothing else. You think the only way for you to make ten is nine plus one. You just gave me five different options."

"Okay, so what are you saying?"

"You need to let go of the fact that you didn't get a first. You're missing the part about the rest of your social skills. Your ability to empathise with people and actually connect. The fact you can communicate, and you are entrepreneurial."

"Well, if I was truly entrepreneurial, I would have got a first."

"How many attempts did it take any of your heroes like Jobs, Musk, Gates, Buffet, etc. to get to where they are? Half of them didn't even have a degree."

This does make a bit of sense. It's annoying, but it does make sense.

He continued, "Just because a lot of people choose to go down one route, doesn't mean you have to or that it's the right choice for you. In these last few months, you have been helping Kaiya, you have been studying like crazy. You've only been at university for like seven months. In the bigger picture, this is nothing."

We got up and carried on playing. Surprisingly I did feel a bit lighter after our conversation. This was a weird time in my life because at school, I would usually fail my mocks but then do well in the real exams. But I'd had a whole year before my exams. Now I had half that time, and when I accepted, the circumstances were harder and more intense, it helped me to forgive myself.

As always though the crackhead decided to make my life a bit more difficult and within a few days of talking to Maaphee, I started feeling sick again. I didn't know what to tell my dad, and he didn't even know I had taken a set of exams already. I was scared, and I felt like a failure, especially after trying so damn hard.

However, something happened that changed my perspective on the entire situation, and that was Kaiya. She told me she had been meditating with Maaphee and that it had helped control her own inner crackhead. I explained to her that my crackhead kept getting upset about my poor performance, but it would then compare what she'd been through and what I am going through right now, and this would make me angry. I would tell myself to stop complaining like a little bitch, especially when I truly had nothing to complain about and try to make myself get over it on my own.

Her response was this: "This lone gunslinger act is unnecessary. You don't have to do this alone. It's okay to ask for help. Also, you and I are not the same individuals, don't think that your problems are any less significant than mine. If they have made you feel this bad, then it's something to deal with."

"But what do I tell my dad? I don't really want to speak to him at the moment."

"Rio, I used to love talking to my dad, and I can't do that anymore. You still have one, make the most of it. When I saw you that day on the train, the night my dad passed away, you were calm, full of confidence and so happy. The way you have been looking in the last eight weeks, I would have thought it was your dad was the one that had died."

Those words changed my thought process in an instant. Kaiya was right. The penny finally dropped. I needed to talk to my dad about how I was feeling and forgive myself for not doing so well. I'd never had to deal with any of this life stuff at school, and actually, it was time to let it go.

Remembering what Saint said too about having everything at the end of university also reminded me that I was a marathon runner, not a sprinter. I had to have a bit of faith, I would get my result, and even though I am here to study, I am also here to have fun and learn about myself.

****

By the time June had rolled around, I'd sat down with my dad and spoken to him on several occasions. I'd decided it was time to forge a better relationship with him rather than keeping everything to myself. I thought of him like a book which only I had access to. The added benefit being this book had an extra twenty-six chapters of knowledge (he was twenty-six years older than me) and I would be stupid to not ask him for help.

El and I were still going strong, and she was really supportive. I wasn't able to secure a summer internship that year, but I started training in the gym again, which helped make me feel better. I realised that sacrificing everything for my grades wasn't the smartest idea, especially after everything that had happened. I finished the year with a high two-one, and I was okay with it. Maaphee was right, my grades weren't going to be the thing that determined how much money I would make. I am.

Manipura
(Solar Plexus Chakra)

FIRE

Kaiya: "If you go to the fridge and see an empty jar next to a full one, which one are you more likely to take?"

Rio: "The only way you don't win is if you don't try."

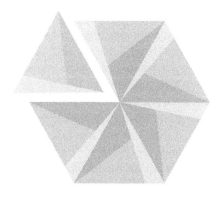

KAIYA ─────────────────────────────────────

Rebirth

It had been over a year since my dad had left me. I had been focusing on developing myself and I didn't want to get into a relationship since Ashley and I split up. I was ready to start dating again and I had three one-night stands (after all a girl does have needs) with both girls and guys.

Being with a guy was completely different from being with a girl, and I didn't really favour one over the other. I was enjoying life, for the first time since Dad had gone, and my formula for university was working. I'd had a friend-with-benefits relationship with a girl and a guy for a while. It was so much fun. (They were two of the one night stands I had previously extended further.) No attachment, no feelings, just orgasms. It was simple and gave me what I wanted, and as long as I was happy, it no longer bothered me if anyone got hurt.

Over the last year or so, I'd had to learn how to accept and forgive myself for certain aspects of my life – something I couldn't have done without meeting Sveekaar and Maaphee. I decided I was going to stop caring about anything which didn't affect me. I would be the one in control, and nothing would affect me anymore.

Alisha and I had spent time over the summer with one another and moved into a house with Maaphee and a new girl called Ahava[18]. She was a girl on Maaphee's course and needed somewhere to live, so we decided to let her rent the other room in our house. The house was great, and everyone encouraged me to go and have a bit of fun and enjoy myself now that I wasn't in a "relationship." Even though Ashley and I never put a label on it, part of forgiving myself was accepting that it

18 *Ahava* = Love (Hebrew)

was my first relationship, but it just didn't work out. There was no judgement, and it felt really good to be in a house that was so open.

In total, I had five one-night stands, three girls and two guys. One of the one night stands was with Alisha, and this happened after Maaphee and Ahava went home for the weekend, and the two of us spent the day together. We went for lunch, then we went bar hopping and the next thing I knew we were having sex. She came out to me over the summer as being bisexual, and after the sexual tension that had built up in my head over the first year, I decided to go for it. The night was amazing, but afterwards, I realised I wasn't in the right place to start anything new, and she also wasn't sure of herself. We didn't want to make living together to be awkward as we had both heard some stories about sleeping with your housemates. Thankfully, we were both mature enough to have this chat and then allowed our friendship to return to exactly that, friendship. (I have thought about that night a lot but I had work to do on myself and my degree, so the last thing I wanted was to feel isolated and awkward in the house.)

Then I was out with Maaphee and Alisha one evening. We were in the smoker's area all talking and enjoying the evening. We were talking about relationships, and who looks cute together when Maaphee said, "You two would make a really cute couple if Alisha was bi." (Maaphee or Ahava didn't know about our little weekend or that Alisha was bisexual. She was still accepting it in her head and understanding it before she decided to make that announcement, and I completely respected that so for him to bring this up was a shock to us.)

"You really think so?" Alisha asked.

"Yeah, you two would have the perfect babies, well if it could work like that. You know what I mean?"

"Well, I guess we'll never know," I responded. Alisha looked unreal that night. Her light eyes against her Latina/African complexion were so attractive, and I really loved being friends with her.

"Look, I'm knackered, so I'm going to get some food and go home. You two still staying out or coming with me?" Maaphee asked.

"I fancy dancing some more. Kaiya will you stay with me?"

"Okay, not too long, but I'll stay. See you in the morning Maaphee."

"Cool, get home safe."

That night it happened again. We were completely in sync with each other's bodies and needs. This was a new level of high. I didn't want this feeling to end. I could feel myself getting pulled in, but I didn't want to. I was scared. I knew I was. But at the same time, I really wanted this. I wanted to be with her. We were best friends, and our physical relationship was immense.

After that night, Alisha was distant. Nothing too obvious to everyone else, but I could tell. Finally, she spoke to me.

"I've been thinking, and it's not fair for us to keep doing this," Alisha said.

"What do you mean?"

"I like you, and I want this to be more, and I know you don't want anything so you and I can't let anything more happen going forward."

Kaiya, be careful now. You can either continue your normal, "Who gives a shit about anyone else?" or handle this differently. Well, the sex is amazing, and I want to have more of it, but I don't want to lose her or make this awkward. To be fair, you're having enough sex at the moment, so sack this off and give yourself an easy life.

"Okay, Alisha, let's stop everything then. Friends and friends only." I could see her welling up, but she agreed that it was for the best and left it at that.

****

I caught up with Rio a few days later and realised he looked quite different. I could tell he wasn't looking after himself and had put on a fair amount of weight. We used to go for a drive around Bath, put some music on and just chat for hours. It was comforting to be around him, but every time he spoke about Elissia, as happy as I was for him, it was really annoying except on this occasion. He mentioned her name, and I didn't feel that kick in my gut and that confused me. *Why is this not annoying me? Do I not fancy him anymore? He has put on weight. Kaiya! Don't be so shallow. Well, it's true, I don't find him attractive anymore. Oh crap, do you like Alisha more than you say you do then... For goodness' sake, here we go. Nope, you're not getting into another relationship. But just think about how much fun she is and how good the sex is.*

"How are you going to let the fear of something that may or may not happen, in this case, a break-up effect the potential happiness you could have now," said Rio.

Why did he have to say that? He is right. I know he's right. See, now I'm confused, do I like this guy or not? I don't like the way he currently looks, but I know he can lose the weight with the right motivation and evidently, Elissia is not giving it to him. Or she is just not as shallow as me. Kaiya, shh, you're going off topic. You like Alisha that much you know, but now it means dealing with your fears.

Rio dropped me home, and that night I told Alisha I was ready to go all in. I was nervous and excited. I had butterflies which was a really good sign but more than anything I felt ready. We told Maaphee and Ahava, and they were both so happy for us. Alisha told me to tell my mum about us as it would be a good way to start the conversation between us two once again. I took her advice and called her to tell her the news. The conversation lasted less than ten minutes, but I had finally reached out to her. This was finally the start of everything I wanted deep down.

A46 to Bristol

By the start of my third year, Alisha and I had been dating for around ten months, and we'd had several arguments along the way. The closer I got to Alisha, the more she became like a drug. I couldn't be without her. I finally got to that point where I could no longer push her away. As far as I was concerned, I was sorted. I had found the person that was right for me. I didn't even think about heterosexual relationships anymore, and I was as content as I could be. Well, when we weren't arguing at least.

Since starting our relationship, we'd spent nearly every single day together. The summer term of our second year was great, and we were fully immersed within the university bubble of life, but I didn't know this. We had most of our arguments over the summer holidays when we weren't together all the time. Whenever we were fighting, I felt the lowest low I could possibly feel. Our arguments seemed to be progressively getting worse. We were bipolar with our relationship. When she would irritate me, dress in a certain way, or if some other guy or girl would flirt with her (not out of her choice), I would always make sure to be flirty with her guy mates. One of them fancied me, so I always made sure to take an interest in what he was doing when I felt angry. I figured the more I did this, the more she would want me, and it would give me that high I wanted. I wanted her to know that I had other choices and that if she didn't work the way I wanted to then things were going to end.

The worst part though, was the relationship drove me to a point whereby even when things were going well, I couldn't enjoy myself. I didn't want to get too high and was always planning how to make Alisha want me more. That's where I got my true high from, her nonstop attention and affection.

***

Alisha moved out in the third year to live with two other girls. At first, I was angry, but I realised that having our own space would also be good. That left Ahava, Maaphee and I together in our quaint three-bedroom house. We only lived a few doors away from Alisha, so it allowed me to come and go as I pleased, but more often than not, we were together.

Ahava and I really bonded in this final year being the only two girls in the house. She was a brunette but feisty as ever. More than anything, she was as blunt as they come. I loved her brutal honesty, no matter how it made me feel. (Okay there were times she was quite harsh, but I learnt very quickly after a few blow-ups that she was only ever looking out for me and this was just her way of expressing herself.)

I'll never forget the day I had just had a big argument with Alisha. When I returned home, Ahava was sitting in the living room relaxing.

"Well, you look awful. What's up?" said Ahava as I walked in.

"Alisha as usual. I think we may need to break up. I'm so sick of these arguments I cannot deal with them anymore."

"What's happened now?"

I explained to Ahava that I was furious with Alisha for changing our plans. We had agreed to have dinner together and then spend the evening relaxing and watching a film. But she wanted to go on a night out with Jessica and Lauren (the two girls she had moved in with). She had invited me to come along, but as I progressed through university, I became more and more aware that I didn't enjoy hangovers and preferred to be fresh for the next day. I enjoyed having a drink and being out with friends, but the pure torture of nursing myself back to health the next day filled me with regret and made me feel awful, so I reduced the amount I started going out in my final year. When I did enjoy a night out, Alisha liked to dress in a certain way. Now I knew it shouldn't bother me, but it always did. Thoughts like: *Look at them ogling your girlfriend. I bet they want to sleep with her. Why is she dressed like she wants attention? Why is she wearing makeup? She clearly wants other people's attention. Why is she talking to everyone else instead of focusing on me? She is meant to be mine.*

The crackhead became far more prevalent in my third year than it had ever before; turning nights I used to enjoy into a constant battle. Drinking helped numb those feelings, but at times it also amplified them even further. It was fifty-fifty.

"Kaiya, I know what you're like, let's go for a drive." She and I quickly put on our baggiest pair of jogging bottoms and hoodies. I normally didn't condone eating when I was sad as I knew that's how I'd put on weight, but I grabbed the half-eaten tub of Ben and Jerry's Clever Cookies with two spoons to take on the journey.

As we descended into the darkness of the A46 towards Bristol, I was able to escape the Bath bubble and felt like I could finally think. Ahava and I, as well as Rio and I, would do this drive a lot, jumping onto the M4 and making a massive loop which lasted about ninety minutes. About twenty-five minutes into the car journey – once we'd had a bit of ice cream and midway through the song chorus of the Black Eyed Peas' "Where Is the Love?" (I know it sounds cliché, but it was one of my favourite songs as a child) Ahava brought up the subject of my dad.

"How do you feel about your dad?" Ahava questioned.

"Fine, I guess… What has this got to do with Alisha and I potentially breaking up?" *Oh, here we go. She is going to say this is to do with my dad, isn't she?*

"Well, you never processed your emotions about him. You just shut it all out of your life."

I continued to stare out of the window while eating ice cream.

"You keep trying to control everything because you're scared of her leaving you. The more you think of this thought and try to protect yourself from getting hurt, the more you're going to push her away. You can't control everything Kaiya, no matter how much you want to."

I turned the music up.

Ahava turned the music down, slapping my hand in the process. She knew I didn't want to hear this, but there was nowhere I could run, we were stuck in a metal box on wheels cruising down the M4 at seventy miles an hour. We both fell silent. *Kaiya, for once just tell her how you feel. You know you always feel better. NO DON'T DO THAT KAIYA! You'll be vulnerable and exposed then! Shut up, I need to talk about this. Take a deep breath Kaiya. Okay, here goes...*

"You're right. I am scared of Alisha leaving me, and is it really so wrong to want to make her want me? I enjoy the attention. It makes me feel really good, but I also know I have to keep her on her toes because that way by her not knowing when I will give her attention, she gives it to me in the hope that I'll give it back to her."

"Jesus Kaiya, you love your mind games, don't you?"

I just laughed because we both knew it was true.

"Kaiya, just try and have an open mind when I say this now, please."

Oh God, what is she going to talk about now? I bet it's Dad again.

"First, let me make this abundantly clear. You, yes you, Kaiya, could not have done anything whatsoever. You physically could not have controlled what happened with your dad."

Knew it. Kaiya wait stop being a smartass and listen. For goodness' sake, she has helped you before, stop being a child!

"It was a random heart attack that could have happened to anyone, but I know you felt like you were out of control. So now every time something doesn't go the way you planned, like this dinner tonight, you get upset and feel like something bad is going to happen. It's not, but if you keep trying to control every little thing and plan for it, you're only going to end up getting hurt."

She is right, you know. Shhh, don't listen to her, Kaiya. Don't let go of the reins, Kaiya, if you do, you'll have nothing! Grip them tighter. We control our lives.

I was lost in thought after that. We continued driving in silence for the next twenty minutes while I tried to digest everything, but I couldn't fathom that my dad's death was still affecting me.

When we got home, I didn't want to be alone, so Ahava got into bed with me and lay there, staring at the glow in the dark space stickers on the ceiling of my room (it always relaxed me looking at the stars).

Finally, Ahava broke the silence, "Kaiya, your dad will take time, but one thing you really need to do is to change the thoughts you tell yourself."

"What do you mean?"

"Well, I've learnt that the brain is hardwired in a certain way. Your thoughts create your beliefs. Your beliefs create your behaviour, and your behaviour creates your habits."

"Okay, go on."

"You are so used to thinking that if you are not the one with the control, you're going to get hurt. Whenever you have a fight like this, or you wind up Alisha and make her a bit jealous, you love the feeling of her wanting you, don't you?"

"Yeah I do, and like I said, there is nothing wrong wanting that attention."

"You're right, there is nothing wrong with someone wanting you but the way you go about it *is* wrong. You don't give yourself any self-love, and you rely on an external source to give it to you instead of doing it from within. I'm telling you this now because if you don't change, Alisha is more likely to end up telling you enough is enough and end it." Ahava grabbed my hand and squeezed it tight. "You know no matter what, I'm always here for you now."

"I know," I said as I closed my eyes while Lana Del Rey's *Lust for Life* album played quietly in the background.

***

By the time December rolled around, a few weeks after that chat with Ahava, Alisha and I broke up. I thought I'd made an effort to change, but Alisha didn't feel that way. The months of having a roller-coaster relationship had finally got to her. This break-up hurt more than my dad's death. I thought I had genuinely found someone with whom I was going to be with. All the chats we had about the future, marriage, kids had all made me feel amazing, but they'd also created a lot of expectations.

The university bubble didn't help either as our arguments all began when we had those few months off during summer. I was home for the Christmas holidays, and I was staying with Rio, and he too had been telling me the same things as Ahava – but now I finally felt ready to listen. Only after losing her, did I realise that I had a lot to change, but I still missed her like crazy.

A lot of it was my fault and accepting that was the hardest thing for me. Ahava told me to think of self-love like this: "If you don't fill your own jar, you will always be needy and reliant on someone else to do so. By filling your own jar and making sure you are always full, you feel better, and people notice this. This is why people are attracted to people who are content and confident in themselves."

That was quite long-winded for me, so when I started thinking of it like this, it stuck: "If you have a fridge with an empty jar and full jar, everyone is always going to take the full one."

To do this, I had to change the words I used. I used to always think that if I didn't control everything, Alisha would leave me but now, I'm telling myself the opposite. It's time I stop trying to plan everything and learn to adapt to the changes that are thrown at me. Sarcasm alert: *Brilliant this should be fun...*

RIO

Man Like E.D.

I started my second year with a fresh perspective. I was going to try and maintain a healthy routine to keep my head strong. I didn't want to feel the same way as my first year, and I was full of optimism that I would achieve the results I so craved. Little did I know that life would slap me and make me it's little bitch.

The hardest thing I'd struggled with over the last few years came back – body confidence. I had put on weight, and it seemed no matter what I did, I wasn't able to shift it. I started training five times a week, eating well but also trying to maintain what I thought was a healthy balance. I thought very wrong. The problems were always amplified when I went home. My brothers started diplomatically enough saying stuff like, "You look… oh um… very healthy," or that I should "change to doing more cardio in the gym." But it wasn't long before they lost all attempt at subtlety: "You need to sort your weight out."

I'd respond: "I am trying! This works for everyone else but me. WHY?!" Before moving on to: "Just shut up, I'm working on it." *You keep saying that and yet you are making no difference in your appearance. You're a fat piece of shit Rio. Sort it out. WTF man.*

I tried not to overthink it, but that crackhead made it impossible to actually let go off these comments. Maaphee kept telling me to let go of my body image issue. Accept that I don't have the right look yet but that I can work on it and change it. As always, I didn't really listen. The more my body didn't change by what I thought was the correct method of losing weight, the angrier I became with myself.

I was walking around a local shopping centre, and I happened to bump into Hihan and Fuan from school. I had noticed them but didn't want to speak to them, so I carried on shopping, but I was still within earshot of what they were saying. It turns out they had seen me too.

"Fuan look. Rio has put on so much weight," Hihan said.

"Oh dear, I wonder if he and that Elisha are still together" replied Fuan.

"I reckon she will probably end it if he doesn't any time too soon. He should really think about how she feels going into public with him."

I tried ignoring it, but I couldn't. I started feeling sick to my stomach. It was upsetting, and it only reminded me how toxic those girls were back at school. I turned around and said, "You two need to shut up. You don't know what you are talking about."

"Oh look, he really is getting angry now isn't he," Fuan said.

"El and I are better than fine, she and I have a great work and sex life together." I felt good saying this because we always had so much fun together.

"What makes you think sex is so good for her. You wouldn't believe the number of times I have had to fake it, just to not hurt a guy's ego," Fuan said.

The two of them were getting to me badly. It was becoming harder and harder to hear all of these thoughts being said in reality. I hated them for saying that, but they were right, there was no way El liked the way I looked right now.

I walked away from this conversation, but I needed to get to the gym. I had to shift this weight as fast as possible, and this is when I began to start panicking. I couldn't breathe. I started feeling light-headed, my heart rate was elevated, and I thought I was going to be sick. I left the shopping centre to get some fresh air and found a bench outside and sat there, calming myself down. *Did El really feel like this and was she just too good of a person to say anything to me? Was I good enough for her now? Rio relax, El isn't like that. Shut up all girls want to look at something nice, what's wrong with you, Rio. Get your shit together.*

I decided to head back to university as I felt like everything was going badly at home. Being back at university made me feel calmer about myself, and I had some time to think. What was I supposed to do? The gym and dieting weren't working, or so it seemed, and I needed a new plan.

I met Saint to fill him in on everything that was going through my head. He reminded me of the bigger picture as always.

"Rio, I know you don't want to hear it but work on your confidence. When you start earning, and you're out of uni, none of this will matter. I know that is where you'll find your natural rhythm for life. Plus a lot of women like success and money, and I don't know anybody with as much drive as you. It's just going to take time."

"Yeah, I need to get back into work mode and just focus on my exams." Had I really not learnt anything? Evidently not.

***

I became more anxious and nervous as the months went on. I started to have issues in the bedroom, but El was completely fine with it. She was supportive but encouraged me to work on my stress and anxiety levels. I had never had this issue before, and I used to be at the polar end of the spectrum where I could always get it up, even without thinking. I felt embarrassed that I had to rely on Viagra at such a young age, but nevertheless, I did what I had to do because I still wanted to have sex.

I also stopped training because all the effort wasn't working, so I didn't see the point in even trying anymore.

One Friday night came by, and El wanted to go out, but I wasn't feeling up to drinking and partying. I knew it would only make me feel more depressed about what was going on in my head, so I wanted to stay away, but at the same time, I knew dancing the night away with El would make me feel so much better, so we headed out to local bars and clubs. Tequila, vodka, Café Patron and Jäger became my entourage that night as on many previous occasions before. We always started with vodka at prees (pre-drinks) with one shot of Café Patron for the road before we left.

As soon as we walked in, it was a shot of tequila followed by a double vodka with Coke. Later as we felt tired, we would have a Jägerbomb followed by another double vodka with Coke. The "deep chats" usually began around 1 am once we were fully licked,[19] and this is when most people normally let out all the shit going on in their head. El knew this is when I would be most likely to open up – something I felt difficult to do otherwise. But even with this endless flow of alcohol flowing through me, I still didn't want to talk. But that didn't stop her from trying.

"Rio, you've not really been the same since you went home last weekend. What's up?" said El.

"Nothing, I've been tired. Usual family rubbish." That was always the easiest way to divert the conversation because she knew as much as I loved my family, they always got on my nerves, my brothers especially.

"Why are you lying to me, I know when something is up. Are you sure it is just about your family?" Evidently, that didn't divert her attention, it only made her examine what was going on with more scrutiny.

"El, look it's just me being stupid and it's man stuff I need to sort out."

"You know as always, you don't have to go through this alone, I am here to support you the way you've always supported me before."

"Honestly, I just need to work this out in my head."

"Rio, why don't you tell me anything. I always have to force it out of you!" She was getting pissed off and frustrated.

"What do you mean. I'd tell you, but it's not a man's place to burden those he loves with his problems, and you really wouldn't understand. Please just drop it."

"You're so fucking misguided – but whatever. You know where I am. Sort your shit out," she said and went to walk away.

I grabbed her hand and said, "Really, why are you getting pissed off?"

---

19 Drunk

"Rio forget it. I don't want to do this now. You don't want to talk, and I cannot be bothered to try and get blood out of a rock."

Well, screw her, you don't need her. This is why men deal with their shit on their own. Oh shut up you're an ass. She's trying to help you, and you don't have the balls to talk to her about what's going on in your life.

El proceeded to walk off and leave me with the drunk, overly emotional crackhead. I just kept thinking about performing the next time we had sex. The anxiety was stressing me out because I figured I had to be a better lover. Otherwise, there was more chance of her leaving me. The stress caused me to seek comfort the only way I knew how – eating food. I left the club and headed for McDonald's. By the end of the night, I was full of regret for eating rubbish food, hate, depression and anger.

A man deals with his shit. You deal with your shit. Stop being worthless. I need to stop being a little bitch. Honestly, how am I getting emotional about shit like this.

This was the classic cycle of hate I was going through in my head. You've all been there, I'm sure when everything is heightened, and it all looks awful.

I stopped going out after that night. I didn't do anything except study and go to the gym as a way of releasing my anger.

Enough is Enough

Over the following months, I had some repeat incidences with not being able to get aroused by El, and it only made my cycle worse. We were arguing more and more, and the inevitable eventually happened while El and I were in my university house. El had been feeling like this for a few months and had tried everything in her power to help me. But by that point, I now realise, I didn't want to be helped"Rio, I can't keep doing this anymore. You're in an endless cycle of self-loathing and no fun. You don't want to go out or anything like that at the moment. You're not the same person I fell in love with."

Was I shocked? Yes and no. I was more surprised that she said it. I thought if it was going to end, I might have had to do it for her. But then again, El was one of the most confident people I knew. This was a fairy tale that I didn't deserve to be living in. If this was a play, I turned up accidentally and managed to get the lead role in the production. Nearly two years later, the production company was letting me go. I just sat there and looked at her with no life in my face.

"If that's how you feel, then it's probably best."

"That's it! You have nothing else to say?" She couldn't believe I wasn't fighting for us. I had truly hit a new low.

"What do you want me to say? Beg you to stay? Tell you I can change? Tell you everything you want to hear?"

"I thought you would have at least made an effort to try and fight for us. I didn't think that you would just accept it."

"Well, I think we are done here. Okay, what is it that I don't do the same anymore then? Yes, I know I've put on a few pounds, but I've been stressed. I can't help it; don't you think I want to help it?"

"You don't want to be seen in public. I have never had an issue with the way you looked. I'm not telling you to watch what you eat or go to the gym. You do that!"

"You tell me every morning to go to the gym."

"That's because you lose motivation all the time. I was only doing it to support you and because you always told me you felt better after you went. You were happier. You're the one who couldn't get over how you looked."

"I'm trying. Sorry, I'm not enough for you then." *This is what she really wants. She wants to say this. She wants to know she is right. Fuck it, just let her know. The only good thing is from this you're going to have an abundance of new motivation to dive into work with now. This is the type of shit the Titans have to deal with so, let's have it then.*

"I'm not doing this with you when you act like a child and don't listen to what I am saying. Your weight has nothing to do with it, you are the most boring and depressing person, and I have tried everything to help you out of it over the last eight months. I need to look after myself now instead of trying to look after you."

Why is she lying? Rio, the fact you've put on weight definitely made this decision easier for her. She is 100 per cent sick of you not getting it up, and you're definitely inadequate in size for her. Fuck her. It's best that she leaves and isn't with us anymore. I wasn't going to say this out loud though and have her confirm my worst possible feelings and insecurities about myself. I already hated myself enough, but this would have been a whole new level. "Just go, El, I don't care anymore."

"Oh, you don't care. This makes my decision a hell of a lot easier." She left the house with tears in her eyes, and I felt like the biggest piece of shit ever. Why would I do that to the one person that had been so good to me? She had genuinely helped me.

Saint heard the whole thing from his bedroom upstairs. He tried comforting me, but it didn't work, so he switched to some harsh truths, ones I didn't want to hear. Saint didn't agree with me that a man has to be of a certain endowment and skillset to please a woman, but I couldn't get this thought out of my head. If a man can't look in shape, then how is he ever expected to attract a female without using money and power?

Rio, you are fat, you are not well endowed, you are stressed and can't get it up. You deserved to be left. You are a joke of a person.

This was arguably the worst headspace I had ever been in. I didn't know how to get out of the funk and to be honest, part of me enjoyed the pain. It was actually comforting. The further I swam out into that sea of pain the more I was able to test if I could bring myself back from it, so the crackhead would help amplify everything in my head which ultimately lead to the real pain of El breaking up with me.

Time for an Intervention

I'd spoken to Kaiya on numerous occasions, and she had told me that I was so misguided in my beliefs that I needed to change my vocabulary. But it wasn't until I spoke to Ahava that I really began to listen.

Ahava's mum was a psychiatrist, so Ahava understood human emotions far more than most of us could at this age. She was also Turkish, so she had learnt how to make shish taouk (chicken shish) and fresh baba ghanoush (aubergine mixed with tahini, olive oil and, in her recipe, chilli and garlic). This dish was phenomenal. We would have it with hummus, rice cooked in butter and grill some fresh halloumi on a hot plate. She was making dinner for herself and Maaphee and invited Saint and me to join them for dinner as Kaiya and Alisha had gone away for the weekend together.

The food was *incroyable*[20] as the French would say. Now with a belly full of home-cooked food, we were about to start watching *The Dark Knight*, but before we did so, I was ambushed into an intervention. Saint, Maaphee and Ahava were worried about me after everything that had happened with El and wanted me to talk about it instead of being a "Buzz Killington" as they described me. It wasn't until halfway through the conversation that Ahava jumped in and unleashed what would become her usual form of blunt honesty.

"Rio, you don't help yourself. It's no surprise what happened," she said.

"Well, you know what, I can't help what happened. I didn't choose for it to happen. I did not choose to put weight on, to get arousal issues (erectile dysfunction) and or performance anxiety," I responded. The entire friendship circle knew what had been happening between El and me, so it wasn't a big surprise when I said this.

"Rio, how many times a day do you call yourself a piece of shit? Or say you're worthless? Or a myriad of other negative thoughts?"

---

20 Incredible

"I don't know, my brain just thinks like that and I'm so sick and tired of trying to fight it. I don't know what to do anymore. I've learnt to like the pain."

"Rio, what the hell, you like the pain?" interjected Saint.

"Okay, Rio, just start by changing the language you use. Just do one thing and try telling yourself one good thing about yourself that you like about yourself," Ahava said.

"I don't like anything," I responded.

"Well, there you go. This was going to happen. You can't love someone else if you don't love yourself first. The thought of you not being good enough leads to you truly believing that. Once you believe that, you try to overcompensate for everything to prove something to yourself and the world. Now the pressure has got to you, and you can't perform, which only makes you feel anxious and stressed out. If you don't change your thoughts, you are never going to change your reality. Look at how your one thought caused you to behave in a way that has now been the downfall of your relationship."

"Don't you think I know this! I know all of this. I have analysed everything from every possible angle and tried to prove to myself that I am capable, and I always fall so short!" This was the first time they had seen me tear up.

"You're still trying to prove something. You don't need to prove yourself all the time! Start by writing down one thing you like or love about yourself and keep reminding yourself of it. What are you grateful for about yourself? Smile, height, body, charm, etc.?"

"Fine, the one thing is my determination and hunger."

"Halle-fucking-lujah," said Maaphee as he applauded sarcastically.

"The kid actually likes something about himself, wow," said Saint. I couldn't help but laugh

"Okay, well, that's a phenomenal thing to be proud off, grateful for and actually something to love about yourself. Every day, you need to do this exercise and write it down on a piece of paper. Remind yourself of it and build new habits of self-love."

"This sounds like a lot of work for something that may or may not work."

"Oh for fuck sake, Rio. Just try it!" yelled Saint.

"Rio, you feel like shit, and I'm offering you a cure. If you try it and fail, you're two or three steps forward. If you try and succeed, you're ten steps forward. This means the only way you don't win is if you don't try."

"If a man isn't in shape, how is a woman ever expected to be attracted to him?"

"Rio, you are so misguided it's not even funny. You need to speak to El about this and forgive her. You have to accept your faults in this relationship. If you don't, you won't get over her, and you'll do the same things again."

"Fact is women like men's bodies, and if you want the best women, you have to have the best body and money. It is quite simple." Saint shook his head in disappointment and Maaphee smacked himself in the face. It was one step forward, two steps back.

"Rio, just think about what I said. You have nothing to lose by trying what I've told you, but everything to gain. Let's leave it at that and watch the film."

We pushed all the sofas together in the living room and made a sofa bed. I remember losing focus because of what they had all just said to me, but at the same time, seeing Christian Bale train as Batman did actually fire me up a bit to get back into the gym.

***

By the start of my third year, my industrial placement year, I finally decided to act on Avaha's suggestions and give it a go. I started working on trying to love myself for who I was, and things did become easier. To get some wind in my sails, the first thing I did was accept my situation and my reality. I was fat and being angry wouldn't change it.

When I started my work placement in July, I joined the gym at work. That and a proper meal plan helped me.

It meant that I finally started losing weight, but it was only when Kaiya noticed that I started to really begin to feel good. My body was finally changing.

While this was going on, it became easier to accept, forgive and love myself. I hadn't fully dealt with breaking up with El, and it still hit me in waves. But I started telling myself how fast my metabolism was. How I love my pure intense determination and my ability to crack jokes at the most inappropriate times.

Ahava was right, reading the old notes I had made on self-love helped me during the periods I felt upset. They allowed my brain to switch from screaming self-criticism to the soothing sounds of self-love. I knew I would have to deal with El, but my ED had not gone away. There were clearly still things I needed to sort out. It had significantly reduced, but my performance anxiety was getting the better of me. Finally, on top of all of this, by December in my placement year Kaiya was single, and so was I. This made me question who was who in my life.

Anahata
(Heart Chakra)

AIR

Kaiya: "Love and hate are not opposites; they're two sides of the same coin."

Rio: "Change your thoughts, change your reality."

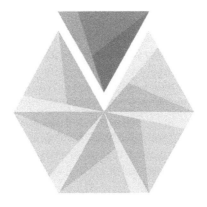

KAIYA

Avalanche

As Easter break approached in my final year, I began reminiscing about how simple life was at school and how it was just Dad and me together. I never really thought about Dad as I just blocked the memory away from my conscious brain. Why live through that pain again and again? Taking some proper time off after being with Alisha and Ashley helped me realise that I was trying to put a square peg into a round hole. The difference was I felt like I had two of these holes, but one could be filled, it just meant doing that one thing I hadn't wanted to do for so many years: come face to face with Megan.

I couldn't remember what it truly felt like to have a mum. I've heard people say "My best friend is my mum," but mine was my dad, and he had been gone for over two years now. I also don't know what it's like to truly stand face-to-face with your demons. To look at them square in the eye and accept and forgive what has happened and move on. Well, for the first time in my life, I decided to stop running away from everything and face that charging bull head-on, and if I got skewered, so be it. I knew I would survive, but it was time. The two of us met in a café for our first dance in what had been an eventful journey up until now.

"Kaiya, I'm so pleased that we finally get to do this. You don't understand how hard it has been for me to sit on the side-lines and wait for you to finally reach out."

"Well maybe you shouldn't have left then, and you wouldn't have been on the side-lines." *Kaiya, calm down, you wanted to reconnect. You knew you could get hurt today, but that's okay. Calm down.* "Sorry, that was rude of me."

"Well, I know you're bound to be upset Kaiya. I know you must still hate me, but your dad and I came to a mutual agreement when we parted. I really wish I could have been there more over the last decade. I hope you can understand that now that you're older and more mature," she replied in her passive-aggressive tone I had learnt to recognise on the few occasions we had met over the years.

You know you don't like it when she uses that tone. Kaiya, breathe. It's fine. Keep Going. "Okay well, I wanted to put this past us, and move on. How's life treating you?"

"It's been fantastic. I've got a book deal on the way, and I've started writing a lot more about how to deal with coming out or making a huge decision like I had to," she said with a smile in her voice.

Her life has been so great without you in it. It's like she never cared about you. "What advice have you been writing about?"

"Well, mostly that if something doesn't feel right, take the leap of faith to do what makes you feel right even if it means there is collateral damage. You'll feel better for it in the long-run."

Wow, Kaiya, you were just collateral damage, and she doesn't even care.

Megan reached over and grabbed my hand, as she continued saying, "Your father was an amazing man, and I don't regret my time with him at all because otherwise, I wouldn't have you. But the decision to leave was simultaneously the best and worst decision I have ever made. I never expected that you and I would have been so distant for so many years."

Her life has clearly been working well since I'm collateral damage it doesn't really matter. No, Kaiya, don't get caught up in this. NO, she has shown me this was the best decision for her. But she also said it was the hardest. DOES NOT MATTER! She left. She chose someone else, and it's like she doesn't even feel 1 per cent of what you have over the last decade. Kaiya, fucking shut up...

I pulled my hand away and made sure I looked her directly in the eye as I responded. I lowered my voice again and slowed down my speech, "Well what was I supposed to do, I was a child whose whole world was shattered and changed. You also don't talk about him. You don't get to. You weren't there for him or me when I was growing up." *Kaiya you said that now stop and reconnect. NO! She doesn't get to abandon you and then make you out to be the bad person.*

"What do you mean I wasn't there? I wasn't allowed to be there!" She began to raise her voice, but only slightly – aware we were in a public place. "That wasn't my doing. That was all yours. Every single time I tried to reach out, you were the one who said no."

"Well, what do you expect when you leave your child and husband for another woman. How is the bitch anyway, the two of you still in love?" *Yes, Kaiya, that's it. Get angrier, Kaiya. Get absorbed into that rage. Hurt her. Make her feel exactly what you had to feel for so many years. Kaiya, this isn't right, you wanted to reconnect. Stop. NO! Keeping going. You are out for blood.*

"Don't you dare talk about her like that. You have never even met her properly or had a conversation with her. Once you get to know Sarah, you'll realise that neither of us are the bad ones in this situation and that life just has some unexpected twists and turns."

"Megan, I don't care what your excuses are, you left us, and it's that simple. It's black and white. There is no grey."

"Kaiya, did you call me here to just make me feel bad about myself and yell at me? If you want to mend our relationship, nothing would please me more, but I'm not going to be your verbal punching bag because you haven't dealt with your emotions about your dad or me." She began to get up from the table.

Wait, she is just going to leave now without even getting to the end of the conversation? What the hell. The audacity of this woman. Last chance, Kaiya, say what you need to.

"Yeah, it's probably best you leave then. You're good at that aren't you."

Megan had a look of incomprehension on her face. I could tell she couldn't believe the words coming out of my mouth. I couldn't believe they were coming out, but evidently, they needed to. "I was getting up to get another drink, but clearly, you are not in the mindset to have an actual adult chat about anything. Maybe it is best if I go and we do this on another day when you're feeling a bit better."

"Bye then." *Look, she is leaving again. She doesn't deal with any of her issues, and I'm the biggest one evidently. Kaiya, just look after yourself and screw the rest of the world.*

"Kaiya, you're acting like a real bitch, you cannot keep blaming me for everything wrong in your life. You have to take responsibility. If you keep hating me, we will never be able to move forward." Then she left.

Kaiya why did you do that? You wanted to reconnect. Fuck that. She deserved it.

The crackhead had grown more ferocious over the last few years, and today I really saw what it was capable of. Even staring at the empty seat opposite me wound me up. I missed having a parent, though. All the times Alisha and I or Ashley and I weren't arguing I always saw them with their mums and how they interacted. I craved that. I wanted it so much, but my craving was blocked by so much anger and rejection.

Later that evening, I got a call from Megan's phone. I was reluctant to answer. However, I did. A concoction of rage and sadness had enveloped me after seeing her.

"What."

"Kaiya how dare you speak to your mother like that. When she got back home, she was in tears, and she told me everything that had happened."

"Wait, Sarah?" *Why is she calling me? Actually, you can tell her how you feel now too, Kaiya. Let it all out on her too.*

"Yes, this is Sarah."

"I'm glad you confirmed that. I wasn't sure how many lesbian lovers, my mum actually had."

"Your mum has done nothing but try to reconnect with you over the last decade, and you have always been such a bitch to her. You don't deserve a mother like that."

"Who the actual fuck are you to tell me what I deserve and what I don't. You need to watch yourself as you are way out of line here. Put Megan on the phone."

"Absolutely not, she doesn't even know I've called you. You apologise to her and grow up. When you do that, that's when she will speak to you next, but I'm not allowing you to make her feel any worse than she already does."

"Bye Sarah, I hope she leaves you as she left me." I hung up the phone and just screamed into my pillow. I was angry at myself for doing that, but every time I heard her voice, all I could see was red. I didn't want to forgive her, I wanted to get even. Before I started spiralling out even further, I heard a knock on the door.

"Go away."

"Kaiya, it's me," said Rio.

"I don't want to talk right now."

"Well, from what half the house just heard, I think you need to talk about it." Rio came in and sat on the bed while I just lay there with my face in the pillow.

I lifted my face out of the pillow, "Rio, I really appreciate it, but I'm not in the mood to talk anymore today. I just want to go to sleep," I said, putting my face back into the pillow.

"I've got a better idea then. I know you don't want to talk, but you've got far too much pent-up energy, and if you don't deal with it, you're only going to get worse. Let's meditate or go for a drive together. You always feel better." Rio had been reading a lot of these spiritual self-help books since he and El broke up and it was something that we enjoyed talking about.

"I don't want to meditate or go for a drive. I want to do something to fully take my mind of it and not talk about it. Let's go out! We always have such a good time, and I could really use a drink."

"Don't run away from it Kaiya, it's not a good idea. Deal with this all now otherwise you won't. I know what you're like."

"Please Rio, let's just go out," I said as I put my hand on his shoulder. "I just want to have some fun and dance, that's it."

"Okay, let's go out then. I have the day off tomorrow anyway."

"Okay, let's go."

The two us hadn't been out since Rio had started his placement. He was looking good, and it was nice to see him smiling, considering all the stuff he had been through with El.

We drank, danced and I forgot about everything. The more I drank, the more I spoke to random people, the more I decided to embrace the cultural "night-out cigarette." The more numb I became, the better I felt.

***

The next morning I woke up with a mouth as dry as the Sahara and feeling like my head was being banged in between two cymbals. I couldn't remember what had happened last night, and I didn't see Rio for most of the day as he used to just sleep through hangovers. I was thinking about everything that had happened with Megan yesterday and how I had treated her and Sarah. I knew I was in the wrong, and while I felt better for getting the poison out, I didn't want to confront the situation again.

Scrolling through my phone, I checked how much I had spent last night, and then I saw the name of a bar I didn't recognise. I tried putting the pieces of last night back together, but it was like an unfinished jigsaw puzzle... And then the main part of the night came to me as clear as my own reflection. I couldn't believe it. I had kissed Rio in this club. My heart began to race, which caused me to throw up. Not because the thought of kissing Rio made me feel sick, but because the panic of what this meant combined with the copious amounts of alcohol caused me to feel very nauseous. I didn't know what to do. Should I tell Rio? But what if he didn't remember? Maybe I should leave it and act like I didn't now. I just wished I could speak to my dad, as he always knew how to make situations like this feel a lot smoother.

Rio woke up later that evening and didn't seem to remember anything, so I decided to leave it. I pushed that thought to the back of my head and decided to head back to university earlier as I had too much going on with Megan and now Rio. I needed the space to just sort my thoughts out.

"Run, Forest, Run"21

The combination of everything that had happened sent me into a panic. I knew once summer was here, I would be forced to see Rio all the time as I was still living with him. This feeling of unease was probably one of the best things to have happened to me as I used this as an excuse to apply for internships in the States. Some of my dad's family lived in San Francisco, and they were more than happy for me to stay with them over the summer. So, once my third-year exams where done, I packed my bags and spent twelve weeks in the USA. Looking back now, this was the only time that running from my problems actually paid off for me.

I took a road trip with my cousins to LA, flew to New York for a few days with work, and had some of the best memories of my life while I was out there. The American guys and girls were also so good looking, and it didn't hurt having an English accent.

My uncle, whose nickname was "Nelly", was one of the craziest people I had ever met, free-flowing with life and would wake up every day at 5 am without fail to meditate before starting his day. I never understood how he was able to do it, especially as some of my nights ended at that time. Nelly really helped me a lot over that summer, and we grew close. He was a fatherly figure in my life again, and I knew I would always cherish my time with him – especially as he helped me calm crackhead's effect on me.

I began meditating with him before work, and it would clear my head, fuel me with energy and set me up for the day. My morning routine would be wake up at 6 am, meditate until 6.20 (I couldn't meditate as long as he could and waking up at 5 am just didn't work for me), then join my uncle for yoga or a workout which finished at 7 am. I felt empowered, like a new woman, with control, but I still had two big issues: Megan and Rio.

---

21 *Forest Gump* (1994). Paramount Pictures.

We took our morning coffee outside on the front patio overlooking the Golden Gate Bridge. As the morning sun was awakening the city, we would chat about the different aspects of life, the way I used to with dad and one day Nelly brought up the topic of love and hate and how they were intertwined.

"What do you mean they are intertwined? Are they not the opposite of one another?" I questioned Nelly.

"Well over the years I have learnt they are actually two sides of the same coin. Love and hate are two things you have to invest in. They can't survive without your emotional investment," Nelly said, demonstrating with a coin.

"I thought hating someone means you don't care about them?"

"Well, the opposite of love is actually indifference. You know you're indifferent about a person or thing when no matter what they do, good or bad, it doesn't affect your emotional state."

"Okay so how do you become indifferent then?" I responded with a puzzled undertone.

"Well, one way is to practice dissolving unwanted emotions or thoughts or what I like to call it 'D.U.E', which is when you remove yourself from any memories or previous feelings you have about somebody."

"How does that work?"

Nelly told me to imagine projecting myself out of my body when I'm remembering or experiencing an emotion I do not like. He showed me this video from *Doctor Strange,* which helped me visualise the process better in my head.[22]

"This actually works?" *No way this works! This sounds like rubbish. Kaiya, stop it. At least try it. Don't judge it until you have given it a go.* I was bamboozled. If this really worked, it would also help me get over the anger I had towards Megan, but I knew it would take some practise. I started practising this daily with my morning meditation and made an effort

---

22 If you want to explore this technique, see the "D.U.E" exercise in Part II, page 167.

to remove and disassociate myself from negative thoughts. I slowly became addicted to it as the combination of the two always gave me a little high afterwards.

Thankfully I was twenty-one and my two elder cousins, Anisha and Amari, were twenty-three and twenty-five when I arrived in the US. They used to visit Dad when we were younger, but this trip really allowed me to bond with them and create really close connections. I had been reading *Everything I Know About Love: A Memoir* by Dolly Alderton and I drew several parallels from it. She says, *"If both parties are aware of the nature of the encounter, casual sex can be really good. If you're using it as an over-the-counter prescription to feel better about yourself, it will be a horribly unsatisfying experience."*

Dolly's ability to be brazen really made me think not to give a shit about what anybody else thinks, but also not to use one-night stands as a way to escape – something I had done after Ashley. More than anything, it made me acknowledge that I didn't actually know a lot about love, and the only way to move forward was to try new things. This combined with meditation and dealing with any form of anxious thoughts empowered me and made me feel, for the first time, as though I had discovered some form of a winning formula to enjoy life. Until now, I had slept with five people, two girlfriends, one other girl and two boys, but since kissing Rio, I wanted to explore the male side of romances more than the female.

The stigma behind girls not sleeping around because they would be considered a slut had made me pull away from situations I might have otherwise embraced. So, on this trip, I decided to "just go with the flow", and after learning very quickly that I could make my anxious thoughts disappear, I was excited to see what adventures would unfold. If I liked a guy and he liked me, I would jump in and do what I wanted. And that's exactly what happened on our girls' trip in LA.

Not getting caught in the disabled toilets in a bar with a five-foot-five dark-haired American guy was one of the most fun and outgoing nights I had ever had. The adrenaline, the anticipation and the sexual tension made the night explosive. (It didn't last as long as I had wanted but it felt amazing to let go of my inhibitions.)

By the end of the summer, I had practised disassociation and meditation daily for sixty straight days. I no longer wanted to set the world on fire, and I knew it would be a great tool in my arsenal to deal with my final year when I got back to university. I felt like it made me more confident too, which helped when I had to deal with anything to do with rejection. Negative words would no longer penetrate my mind; they bounced off me. Any time I became stressed at work, or negative thoughts appeared in my head, I just dived deep into my head for ten minutes or so, and it was like I was reborn.

What was even better was that I'd had a total of four random one-night stands that either ended in a toilet, on the beach or back at their place. The beach night was probably the best as Anisha, and Amari met me afterwards, and we enjoyed watching the sunrise together. The sand between my toes, the wind coming off the shore and the afterglow of a rogue one-night stand combined with the buzz of marijuana gave me the perfect ending to my time there.

It's Going to Take More Than Time

It had been nine months since I had spoken to Megan. After I came back from the States, I was in a really good headspace, and I didn't want to ruin that. Seeing Rio wasn't as hard as I thought it would be, but I knew, even if anything happened, I would be okay and I could deal with it. I didn't want to speak to Megan yet, but as Christmas came closer and closer, I realised I didn't want to start another year in the same position.

Finally, as Christmas break approached, I reached out to her to meet me in the same café. I wanted to make amends for what I'd said to her and Sarah. The three of us sat down together.

Okay, Kaiya, we're not going to have a repeat of last time. Everything is going to be okay. Breathe and know you're taking a really big step today. I'm proud of you. I had been practising more self-love instead of getting angry at everything so quickly.

"Megan, I have to apologise for how I have behaved over this last decade but especially since Dad died. I wasn't ready to deal with his death, the break-ups, university, or anything for that matter. I realise now that I hurt you as much as I was hurt, if not more and I did that maliciously. I hope you can forgive me for that. Sarah, I also have to ask you to forgive me for the way I spoke to you on the phone, and I hope that you and I can start fresh because I've seen how important you are to my mum. So that means, I need to show you the same level of respect." *Go on Kaiya, well done.*

Sarah and Megan looked shocked. To be honest, so was I. I didn't expect to be apologising to Sarah.

"Kaiya, I don't know what to say. I cannot believe you've just said all of that. How? What happened to get you from where you were to where you are now?" Megan asked.

"I've started being kind to myself and fully accepting the past for the past. Seeing Uncle Nelly in San Francisco also helped me a lot too. He helped me realise that no matter how much I think about it, I cannot change it." Mum and Sarah both had smiles on their faces.

"Did you know that love and hate aren't the opposite of one another?"

"No, I didn't," Megan said.

"Neither did I. The opposite to love is actually indifference. I always thought hating you meant I no longer cared, but actually, I realised that my hate, while somewhat justified in the beginning when I was a child, is not acceptable now. Dad is gone, and I'm far more accepting of that, and I want to have one parent in my life at least. So, I hope we can start rebuilding this relationship now, Mum."

"Did you just call me Mum?"

"I did, I'm finally ready to have a mum again. In fact, I actually want one now. Maybe even two mums if I'm lucky?"

Mum and Sarah started crying. What an absolute relief I felt. I was feeling high like I had never felt before and I couldn't believe it. We ended up sitting there for hours afterwards.

***

Rio had told me that everyone thinks that time heals wounds, and this was something I used to think too, but he said they were mistaken. He gave me this example: if you have a broken leg and just leave it to heal without doing any physio work, it won't heal properly. It will heal crooked, wrong or weak. The physio is what helps strengthen the leg and allows it to heal in the right way and in the correct position, but it takes time and effort. I hadn't been doing the physio with my mum and working on our relationship. Once I was able to accept my responsibility within the relationship and how my behaviour was not okay, combined with the habits I had now developed, I was starting to look at life from a whole new perspective. I was slowly working my way through all of my issues and also started seeing a therapist. Again, this was Rio's idea, and he told me to look at therapy as my physio. Turns out I had always had the wrong perspective of therapy and assumed you had to be fully broken, a narcotic abuser or something along those lines to use it. How wrong I was. The only issue I still wasn't sure about was how to speak to Rio about the kiss.

RIO ————————————————————————————————————

Paid Learning

After breaking up with El and adjusting to the working world, I found it harder than anything else that I had previously known. My mum was the reason behind my creative side, but it was my dad who helped me get some business acumen from a young age. Drip feeding me knowledge since I was ten, I had enjoyed learning about basic business principles. This, combined with everything I saw from the Titans, drove me further down the path of wanting to be an entrepreneur which is why I found it hard to work under somebody else.

My brothers and sister were away for the weekend, and I was sitting down for breakfast with my dad one morning at the start of the placement year when I brought up this topic. We had really grown a lot closer than I had expected, especially after what Kaiya told me. My brothers were still assholes, but nowhere near as much. Either they were changing, I was, or it was the combination of the two.

"Rio, how has work been? You know I'm so proud of you for getting a job on your own and everything you have been doing." This was really nice to hear from him. I felt good about getting the job at Puma as it was something I never expected and did on my own.

"Thanks, Dad, but I really don't like it. The work is boring, and I want to do something else. I feel like leaving."

"But you enjoy learning, don't you, Rio?"

"Yeah, I've realised I do, but only when it is relevant to helping me earn money." What was the point in learning something if it didn't help me get to a place of financial freedom? That was my goal, after all.

"Okay, look you've got this chance at Puma to work and design the way you've always wanted. Just because the job isn't quite what you wanted it to be, change it up."

"How can I change it? I get given work that I don't enjoy."

"This is where you discipline and train your mind to push through the stuff you don't like. The same way I'm sure you've had to at university with modules you didn't like."

"Okay, that makes sense, but how do I actually enjoy work?"

"That's very simple. Your perspective right now is, 'Go to work. I'm bored. I don't like it. The work is not what I want to do, etc.'?"

"Yeah…" I said, nodding in agreement while sipping my morning coffee.

"Okay now think of it like this. Every day you go into work, try to learn one new thing. It doesn't matter what it is but try and learn one new thing. You are there for twelve months. You are not quitting or leaving. Think of it as being paid to learn. Remember you don't have to be there for your whole career, you can go anywhere else, but think about the doors this will open for you because Puma is on your CV."

"Paid learning?"

"Exactly, you're getting paid, and you have to be there. You might as well learn as much as you physically can as you never know where it will help you later in your life."

That conversation was one I would never forget and changed my entire year. From feeling sluggish and bored, my perspective changed, and so did my vocabulary. Looking back, I realise that it was the combination of the two. My work life within a few months shot up instantly. I started working on other projects I liked, helped upskill my team, and I felt amazing and excited to go to work every single day. It was a new me and all it took was a simple perspective change. That is when I realised that instead of changing my outer world, I changed my inner world and all of a sudden, I was having fun with life again. I changed my thought, and as a result, my reality changed too. I loved that quote so much that I even got it tattooed on me.

Things Just Got Better, FFS

During my last few months of second year at university, I took the bold step to seek out a counsellor. I didn't know what to expect. All I knew was that I didn't like the way I was living my life and how I was feeling. I only had a limited number of sessions with her, but in my first session, I immediately had a breakthrough. I loved it. It took a few months for me to find the right one, but once I settled in at Puma, I discovered they had their own in-house counsellors.

As you know, I'd always perceived that my problems were never that big compared to what Kaiya had been through. Whenever I would compare anything going wrong in my life to either death, tragic illness or anything of that drastic nature, it always reminded me not to worry about the small shit in life. It was a good perspective check. The issue was though it also belittled my ongoing long-term problems as I would brush them away as if they were nothing. I would end up pushing it to the back of my head and not dealing with them, only for them to come back later, and the cycle continues.

I look at counselling as something that doesn't mean you are broken or weak. More as an unobjective perspective on my situation. My friends and family were great for talking to, but at the end of the day, they were slightly biased because they knew me. Counselling let me talk about anything without any worry of being judged. As a result, whatever it was I was going through then, after speaking to the counsellor, I usually went and told my friends and family. It gave me space to think and bounce ideas off another person.

I met a girl at work named Shreya. She was amazing. Warm, bubbly and full of life, but she had her own issues too. She and I became very close, and since I had been losing the weight, she had been noticing me more and more. It had been around eight months since El and I broke up, and I was ready to start seeing girls again and even having a relationship.

Shreya and I had spent the night together (nothing happened except for kissing) but we spoke for hours, listening to music and relaxing. I hadn't felt this way in ages.

Finally, after a few months, the two of us actually hooked up, and to my surprise, my ED didn't affect me at all. I didn't need my little blue pill. I was so happy. The problem was I thought we would hook up again and again, but it was only that one night and I was nervous as hell. I didn't perform the way I had wanted to because I was in such shock that a girl as good looking as her wanted to sleep with me. She could have had anyone. El was stunning too, but for whatever reason this girl was different. She was older, entrepreneurial, passionate, athletic, loved Marvel, and we fit together like hand in glove. This escalated the crackhead's comments on my endowment and made my performance anxiety worse.

One day I decided to take my laptop to this café I used to frequent during lunch and work. They served the best chicken shawarmas, and I got to know the guys there so well they would always give me a little piece of baklava on the house. This was an end of week special I loved.

On this particular Friday though, my sanctity for creativity and relaxation became one of hell due to hearing the voice of a narcissistic piece of toxic waste.

"Is that little Rio?" I wasn't sure who had said that as it had come from my five o'clock.

"Ohh. Hi, Hihan. What are you doing here?" I said as she walked over to my table.

"I work around here too. How have you been? Are you and El still together?" Hihan enquired as she leered at me over her paper coffee cup.

Rio, lie. Just say, yes. But if I lie and she knows this will only be worse. Oh, please just walk away. F' it, just respond, it may make this go quicker. "No, we're not together anymore."

"Oh really, that's interesting. Let me guess it was the height thing."

"Actually, no it wasn't, and if you don't mind, I've got work to do so…" I looked down at my designs to carry on working.

"You always were so easy to wind up. Let me guess what it could be? You were always insecure about your height, your weight, well your whole personality. Perhaps the issues lay within the bedroom?"

"Nope, it wasn't that" I responded looking back up at her. "Please, I've got to work now," I said gesturing to my designs.

"Your mouth is saying one thing, but your face is saying something else. Well look, Rio, just remember there is always surgery if you need to make it… you know… bigger. I'm sure you'll find someone who likes your length of endowment."

"Nice to see you haven't changed, Hihan," I said.

"Anyway, while this has been fun catching up, I've got things to do," Hihan said as she walked away.

Hihan had really struck a nerve with me. She knew my worst thoughts and somehow laid it all out in front of me. I had always assumed I would get another chance with Shreya, but that never came. I started overthinking a myriad of thoughts and felt jealous when she wouldn't hang out with me but met up with other guys. What was worse, when she did show me some attention, I felt amazing for the rest of the day, but if she didn't, I wondered why. I started to feel anxious daily as I didn't know how to act around her at times. She wouldn't ignore me, but we would make plans, I would get really excited and then she would cancel with some form of an excuse at the last minute. I never knew what to say except for "Oh okay." I hadn't felt this way about a girl in a long time, so I did what I'd learned to do when I'm sad which was avoid overeating and put all of my energy into gym and work.

You can probably guess that this only made her pop into my head even more. I started using Maaphee's disassociation of memories technique, and it really helped during this time, but still walking around the building always filled me with some form of anxiety. My emotions were all over the place, despite trying to find new ways to look at situations. The counsellor described her as my cocaine, and I was hooked. I needed a hit every single day and working in the same building as her made it so hard to stop being an addict as I knew it was always readily available for me and nearby. Every time I saw her, I thought, "Was I big enough? Could I have been in better shape?"

The one thing that always ignited the fire in my belly when I felt down was to go outside and just stare at the building. Think about how amazing this opportunity was, and then people watch while listening to music. It would recentre my focus on work so I could work for hours on end. The best part was always working through the day late into the evening when the office was empty. I got some of my best work done at those times. By the end of the year, I knew this would pay dividends, but I had to learn to stop letting her dictate my emotions.

Gaining Clarity

Shreya had been messing with my head a lot recently, and I was sick of it. I kept trying to do things to get her attention. I thought by being a good sounding board, that being a motivating individual in her life, I would win her over to be my girlfriend. None of that worked. She would do something, and it would make me feel euphoric or sad for the entire day. The crackhead would be unbearable, and I would always have this gut-wrenching feeling. The counsellor told me that I couldn't control what Shreya was going to do, so it was down to me to control how it affected me. She was absolutely right, but no matter how hard I tried, her actions always got the better of my emotions. Then finally I got clarity.

The sun rose on a Saturday morning as the dew began to slowly evaporate. The golf course was in phenomenal condition: fast greens, smooth fairways and perfect bunkers. The final of the tournament began, and it was match play – Brooks vs Rio.

Brooks had become one of those guys I loved to play against as it brought out the best in me. I had to be focused and in my element. If I wasn't, he would win every single time. Brooks was also my cousin which made me want to beat him even more. What I thought was going to be the equivalent of the battle in the sun (the classic match of Jack Nicklaus v Tom Watson at the 1977 British Open) was changed to the battle of the heavens. By the fifth hole, the sun had disappeared behind a wall of black clouds. Next thing the heavens unleashed themselves all over the course. The combination of torrential rain and wind created a cyclone that meant every single shot we took required our full concentration.

As soon as the rain came, so did a smile on my face. I knew everybody hated playing in the rain, and so did I, but because I knew everybody else hated it, I began to love it. I wanted to win. After an absolutely shitty start and continuously being on the back foot the whole round, I was finally able to break through on the ninth when I made an eagle. A jolt of electricity went through my body. I was pumped. The adrenaline was flowing. I imagined this is what it felt like to be on cocaine (I have never done it so I wouldn't know), but I had clarity like I had never felt before.

The final nine holes of the round were some of the most fun I had ever had. I had to stay focused on the present. When self-doubt struck, I had to forget every bad shot that had happened before and remember the good ones. I knew I could do this; it was just about playing within myself. By the time the sixteenth had arrived, I was two holes down with three left to play,[23] and I had to do something otherwise, Brooks would have bragging rights on me forever. The rain had picked up on the fifteenth hole, and water was dripping from my cap. There was no time to think before each shot, just pick up the club, stay focused and just commit. That's it. *Whatever you do, f…ing commit.* With the sixteenth being a drivable par four, I went for it. The ball flew as straight as an arrow, as if I was throwing a dart, which helped me take it to one down with two to play. On the seventeenth, I saw Brooks had messed up and knew if I could hit this shot half decent I could win the hole. I hit one of the purest shots I've ever struck leaving me with a tap in to make it all square walking on to the eighteenth.

I had never had so much adrenaline running through my body, to the point I thought I may have been sick, but at the same time, I loved it. Three, two, one – boom! I launched a driver on what is known as the *Tiger line*[24]. When we got up to the fairway, we couldn't find my ball initially. I shat myself. We looked and looked, with every second passing by, my heart moved closer and closer into my stomach. Then as the end of my three-minute search time was upon me, within a ditch, in thick shrubbery, I found my ball.

Are you joking, I've hit one of the best shots of my life, and this is what happened? Typical. Shut up. Breathe. Just make a clean connection and give yourself a chance. Breathe.

---

23 Three points left to grab, and currently losing by two, so if I win all three holes, I'll win by one point.

24 The most dangerous path to the hole, usually over trees or some form of hazard. If you hit it well, you're in an A1 position but if you miss it, you're in trouble.

I hit one of the best shots destroying the shrubbery as my club impacted with the ball. The crackhead immediately decided to start celebrating. *We can win this! Come on, that's it one-putt. You've got this. It's easy. Be quiet! Rio, breathe. Focus. You still have to hole this.* I controlled my breathing, hit the putt and low and behold it rolled in. I genuinely couldn't believe what I had just done. It felt as if this script had been written beforehand, I was in that much shock.

Brooks and I shook hands, smiled and then I went over to my dad and gave him a massive bear hug. I knew this would always be one of my favourite sporting moments – the competitiveness, the focus and the fact that I had to continually stay in the moment. The balcony of the clubhouse was full of other members watching us. My dad had been walking around with me the whole round as he used to when I played junior golf. Having him watch me win meant so much to me. I was never going to be a professional, so this was the closest I was going to feel like Tiger Woods, and I loved every moment of it.

I learnt a lot about myself that day, not just about my resilience, but about staying in the present and focusing on the moment. I didn't let the crackhead get the better of me as it had done so many times before. It brought me a sense of euphoria and calmness that helped me realise, I can do what the counsellor told me. Every time I hit a good shot, and the wind blew the ball offline, or it had an unlucky bounce, the crackhead went off, but I calmed it down and focused on the next shot. I didn't let it affect me, and this was something that had always ruined my golf game before . Finally, I had clarity, and it helped me realise that I can actually deal with my emotions.

Dreams or Flashbacks

Kaiya was on Easter break and still staying with us. We hadn't seen one another since Christmas, and it was nice to come home from work and hang out with her.

I thought I was going to have my second chance with Shreya as we'd planned to spend the day together and then I was going to go back to her house for the night. I was like a child waiting for Christmas Day to arrive only to find out on Christmas Eve that Santa wasn't coming. Shreya had double-booked with a friend before she had booked the day with me. This was her favourite excuse, but this wasn't the main point, so let's continue. I came home from work on a Thursday afternoon and remember hearing crying from Kaiya's room. I knew she had gone to speak to her mum that day, but I wasn't sure how it had turned out, so my initial reaction was, "Oh shit." Kaiya never really knew of Shreya, and I liked it like that. I had kept it quiet from her, and the only people who knew of her were Saint and oddly enough, my dad.

Kaiya didn't want to take any of my suggestions for meditation, dealing with problems straight away etc., and suggested we go on a night out. To be honest, when she suggested it, I was quite happy to just get away and feel like I was back at university again. I got absolutely obliterated. I was licked to the point I couldn't remember anything, and the next day I was hanging like an old man's testicles. I vaguely remember mentioning Shreya and kept having faded flashbacks, but nothing detailed. The only thing I can remember was the scent of Black Opium as Kaiya wore it that night. My head was even more screwed up the following week as Kaiya decided to go back to Bath after the night out. From having dreams about Shreya, I started having odd dreams about Kaiya. It was always the same. Us two sitting on a bench, laughing and chatting then she leaned in, and we started to make out. It always felt so real, but I never told her about it.

***

117

The counsellor was good, but I felt like I needed to make more progress quicker, so I decided to seek out a CBT (cognitive behavioural therapy) and psychodynamic therapist. Her name was Kate. With my counsellor, we only dived into things I felt like talking about, whereas with Kate, I had to look into topics of my past I never thought were relevant but actually were.

My counsellor was a man, so it was slightly easier to talk about sex stuff, however, I needed to be able to be open and upfront with any issues. Also, as someone who still felt intimidated by women, I thought if I can talk to a woman about my deepest darkest secrets, I should be alright talking to any woman.

I have an incredibly high sex drive, so especially in stressful times, I watched a lot of porn. This was the hardest (excuse the euphemism) aspect to talk about with Kate. I had never spoken about it with anyone before.

Kate's office was small and quaint. It felt homely with its smell of lavender, and she had a sofa which was a bit too small to be a two-person sofa but big enough for any size person to be comfortable on.

We dived into the world of porn, masturbation, the effects on your brain, dopamine and more. The type I watched, how it made me feel when I first started, and so much more. The repeated theme of stress and masturbation were highly correlated in my case

"Do you regularly masturbate?" enquired Kate as I sat in her office trying to face some of my own demons.

"I can go a week without doing it, but then at other times I could do it every evening after work."

"What about masturbating without porn?"

"I mean I've done it before, but it is not as enjoyable. Essentially what happens is I think of Shreya. I miss her and want her attention. Then I think of the night we slept together. I then remember I didn't perform like I wanted to. This then reminds me of the issues I had with El and how it caused us to break up. She says it isn't, but I know deep down it is. I then watch porn to de-stress and feel better, but then the cycle restarts if I keep thinking about Shreya or El."

"Let's park porn and Shreya to one side. We will tackle this, but let's break it up. This is something new you have brought to light about your time with El. Why do you think that she broke up with you because of your performance anxiety?"

"I don't think it is just that. It also well my... size and the ED."

"ED?"

"You know…"

"I'm afraid I don't."

"Are you actually going to make me say it? Fine, erectile dysfunction."

"The reason I want you to say it is because it means your accepting and owning it. Right now, you're carrying around a lot of shame with you and shame is one of the worst emotions of all. When you are shameful of something, you don't want other people to know about it because it makes you feel awful. Imagine a pot full of steam. If you keep the lid on and hide it, the steam will be trapped, but if you open it and let it out the steam will evaporate and leave. Your body is the pot, and the shame is the smoke. Now just by you talking about it with me, you are slowly accepting it and removing that lid."

"Okay, but what do I do about all of this?"

"Reducing the amount of porn, you watch can help but also come to accept that you will never know if El is actually lying to you or not. The same applies to Shreya. In her eyes, you two may just not be compatible, and that's the harsh part of life. You can never know what is going on in their head, only yours."

"See, up until the last six months or so our sex life was great, that's why I think it was all down to that," I said.

"You don't think your behaviour changed in any other way besides that?"

"Well, I put on weight, and I didn't really want to go out."

"You've told me she always said the weight was never an issue, but you couldn't believe it to be. Not being the fun and energetic person like you were at the start of the relationship seem more like what the issue is. You let your stress manifest into something that caused all of these issues."

"Have I overthought everything?"

"Seems that way."

Every time I saw Kate, I knew a little bit of me was improving, and I loved it. It got to the point when if bad things happened, I would walk straight in and tell her exactly what had. She didn't have to force it out of me.

A New Beginning

El had graduated and was working in London, but before I went back to uni for my final year, I thought about reaching out to her so we could talk. Kate was right, and the more I let that session sink in, the better I started to feel better about myself. Every time I thought about the issue, I disassociated my memories and changed my thoughts.

El and I met at the café for lunch. I knew she loved Turkish food, so I thought this would be a nice place to break baklava and move on from the past. When I saw her, she looked amazing – black jeans, with black boots, a white blouse and a red jacket. I always loved that outfit.

"Congratulations on graduating, El. Thanks for meeting me today, I know you didn't have too," I said

"It's okay, thank you, and how have you been?" responded El.

"Better now, thanks. I'm just going to get straight to it as I realised you had every right to act the way you did, but I just want you to know, you will always be one of the greatest things to have ever happened to me. I do have to ask though, was our sex life at all a part of the reason we broke up?"

"Rio, that means a lot to me, and I genuinely hope everything has been working out for you and honestly, it really wasn't. I'm not just saying this to make you feel better. You need to have some faith in yourself like you did at the start of our relationship. If I really had an issue with that, do you think I would have stayed with you for as long as I did?"

"Hmm, that's true. We did have a lot of fun, didn't we," I said with a cheeky grin on my face.

"Exactly, I've been with other guys since we split up and nobody ever gave me as much attention as you. It made me feel amazing, and I appreciated what we had even more," she said sincerely.

"Really, that's interesting."

"Honestly, the person you became is what changed it for me and what I did was selfish upon reflection… but if we'd stayed together with you in that state, I would have ended up resenting you. My whole time at university would have just gone past me and been spent looking after you."

She was right. It was nice to hear what she was saying, and I didn't have that gut-sinking feeling as we were talking about this. When I heard her say that she had been with other guys, I thought it would have triggered me, but actually, I was happy for her. That was one reaction I absolutely did not expect. El and I continued to chat for a while, and I could tell things had changed inside both of us. Having gone through all the experiences during my work year, I could feel my confidence growing.

I had a very different set of beliefs throughout my final year. I didn't want to go back to Puma, but I made sure to apply to several graduate schemes to give myself the best possible opportunity for securing one. Nothing had stuck by January, but it didn't bother me because I knew I was capable of getting one. Puma really gave me a lot of confidence to know that I enjoyed working and performing in the real world. I knew I could do it. I gave a presentation to my entire division (200 people) in my final week, and it felt amazing to see the culmination of all my work and efforts being appreciated. Shreya left Puma around that time too, and actually never said goodbye except by text. It was strange not saying goodbye to her, but also showed me what type of person she was. I was happy to finally be away from all that cocaine (Shreya) and rehabbing myself at university.

By January I was almost halfway through my final year at Bath. I was still seeing Kate (video call as she was in London) and all my closest friends and family now knew I was seeing a therapist and had seen a counsellor for over a year – and they were all really supportive. Their first reaction was to fear the worst. Still, after explaining how I was using therapy as an unobjective new perspective on certain situations, they too realised that actually, the societal stigma around it is very wrong. Feeling empowered, calm, and knowing I only had six months left until the closing of this chapter, I was determined to make the most of it.

Vishuddha
(Throat Chakra)

SOUND

Kaiya: "You are the observer. You are not the emotion."

Rio: "Stop fighting life. Surrender and move with it."

KAIYA ————————————————————————

Fifty Minutes of Learning

In the months leading up to graduation, Mum and I became really close. This was the best our relationship had ever been, and I began to see her not only as a mum but also as a friend. The more time I spent with her and Sarah, meant that I also grew closer to Sarah and saw how much the two of them really loved one another – which only emphasised that the divorce was just a part of my life. I still think about my dad and would have loved for him to see how far Mum and I had come. Sunday mornings now consisted of breakfast waffles, eggs benedict combined with vast amounts of English breakfast tea (Sarah was a professional chef) and it became one of my favourite ways to spend the weekend.

Everything was going well. I had a job lined up in London with the same company I'd worked for in San Francisco. I was happy with my friends and family, and my friendship with Rio was great. That's when life decided to through me a curveball.

Three days before our Graduate Ball, I received a call from the company informing me that the position I was supposed to be filling in London had been moved from the London office back to the main San Francisco headquarters. They offered me a London position, but it was a different role with significantly less pay. I had fourteen days to make my decision if I wanted to move back to San Francisco for the next eighteen months or if I wanted to be unemployed and search for a way to start paying back all the student debt I had collected over four years. (Dad had left me some money when he passed away, but I couldn't touch it until I reached twenty-five and only use it to buy some form of real-estate. He wanted to make sure I would always have a roof over my head no matter what and as small a mortgage as possible. Even when he was gone, he was still looking after me. Thanks, Dad.)

Moving to San Francisco wasn't in my plan; not part of the journey, I thought I was supposed to be on. I was comfortable and happy working in London, but the more I thought about San Francisco, the more I could see this was an opportunity I would potentially regret if I didn't take it. I didn't want to take the London role, I wanted the San Francisco role, but in London. My anxiety levels grew immediately like the mercury of a thermometer in hot water. Meditation only reduced the effect slightly. I didn't know what to do. I was at such a crucial point in my relationship with my mum and Sarah, I didn't want to put the brakes on the momentum. I had wasted far too much time being angry, and I was determined to catch up as much as possible.

At the same time, as graduation approached and having the new mindset of tackling my problems head-on, I wanted to make sure I spoke to Rio about the kiss before university ended. When the chapter came to a close, I needed to make sure I had said everything I wanted to.

My therapist, Lucia, had been helping me through this time, especially as I had embraced therapy and actually began to look forward to it. She was helping me loosen my grip on trying to control life, but every time I got close to letting go, the crackhead would speak up. Learning to become familiar with the unfamiliar was much harder than I thought, but I knew it was something I had to embrace. I knew every time I stepped into that room, I was going to learn something new about myself, and it was exciting to do a deep dive into my consciousness.

Lucia had this one-and-half-person sofa that I would get comfortable on. There were always three pillows, and I would plant my feet firmly on the ground, place one pillow under each arm and hold the final one next to my chest. Her office always smelt of vanilla and had such a calming atmosphere. Her dark hair coupled with her geeky glasses and smile always made me feel warm and welcome. I hadn't told anybody else about the job opportunity, but here I could share my thoughts about San Francisco and how it would impact my relationship with my mum as well as the fact that I needed to speak to Rio.

"Okay, Kaiya, you've brought a lot into this session so let's dissect it bit by bit. Putting your relationship aside with your mum and Sarah, why are you hesitant about going to San Francisco?"

"My biggest fear is what happens if I get fired, and I am unemployed in the states living with my uncle and auntie. I don't know if I am good enough to compete in the adult world. The internship was fine because I knew I was a student, so they couldn't expect that much from me." I continued explaining how the crackhead had made me feel like I may fail, and this was something I had never really felt before. How my anxiety was at its highest when I should be looking forward to one of the best days of my life.

"Also, if things work out with Rio, I'd love to work in London here with him, my family and everyone, even if it meant less pay. Even when I was in the States, I missed him. I wanted to tell him everything that was happening, but I held back because I wasn't sure how to deal with it all."

"Kaiya, how did you fare with your internship? You didn't get fired, you actually got offered a job, didn't you?"

"Yes, I did."

"So, what makes you think you're not good enough? You have proven to yourself that you are good enough. You are capable of competing in the adult world. You need to keep reminding yourself of that. Set your screensaver as the contract you have been given. Use it as a reminder to reinforce that you are good enough to yourself. If you weren't, you would not have been given that contract."

"I love that idea, okay. But what about Rio?" I was praying she would have an answer for me. A concrete step-by-step guide on how to deal with this issue that had been on my mind for nearly fourteen months now. Am I really going to make a career decision over a boy? I know I like him; I wouldn't think about him so much if I didn't. He has been through so much with me and has been my rock for so long. Why would I want to leave him?

"I can't tell you what to do about Rio. Take some time to reflect, but if you do want to talk to him and tell him, remember not to build any expectations in your head about how he will react. Don't try to control it. You can't control what he is going to say, so remember that if you decide to tell him."

This wasn't the answer I was looking for. How was I supposed to not build expectations? Going back to San Francisco would be amazing too. I improved so much in twelve weeks, being there for eighteen months would be life-changing.

Opening up to Lucia was one of the hardest things I have ever had to do. Learning to be comfortable with that vulnerability and exposure made me feel like an open wound every week for fifty minutes. I hated that, but at the same time, I loved the relief that I felt at the end of every session. Therapy had always seemed strange to me as you had to open yourself up to a random stranger.

At first, I would go in there only talking about small, petty arguments, and briefly discussing my mum. Lucia said I'm definitely more of a flight person as opposed to fighting, and she was absolutely right. I ran from everything for so long, but that is why I was here, because I was tired of running. Look how long I have run from Rio.

Lucia had really been an amazing teacher in helping me learn the tools to digest and dissect my emotions. Through meditation and Lucia, I realised the crackhead would just go on incessantly through my life unless I learnt to control it. I didn't want another repeat of that day when I lashed out at my mum or Ashley and made them feel awful because I was projecting my emotions on to them. This is why Lucia was in my life now, and I'm glad I actually listened to Rio when he suggested it instead of being my usual stubborn self. It was only during my meditation or when I was listening to music that I can enjoy some blissful silence instead of hearing the crackhead. I'm glad though that I was finally aware of it so I could actually hear some of the rubbish that the crackhead went on about instead of thinking it was actually me.

Graduation

Graduation day arrived. Four years of hard work had culminated in achieving a first in my masters and receiving a job offer from a top publishing firm. Our graduation ceremony was amazing, both Mum and Sarah came to watch it. They headed back that afternoon as we all started preparing for the Graduate Ball.

Maaphee, Rio, Sveekaar and Ahava had already graduated and been enjoying their day. Alisha graduated the same day as I and we were both in a place where we were finally able to be friends without any old feelings. I had truly become indifferent to her, but I was so grateful that she had been part of my life. She was seeing someone new, and as time went on, we stayed in contact. We had been such a big part of one another's life. It was amazing to be in a place where I could control my feelings.

When the time came, I introduced her to my mum and Sarah. She had always wanted me to reconnect with them so it was nice to let her know that if she hadn't broken up with me, I wouldn't have started trying to get my act together and not become emotionally dependent on others to "fill my own cup." The evening drew in, and we were all dressed up, ready for our final night together. Rio and I were outside together in our student union reminiscing over a few drinks during the grad ball.

"Rio, so you know that I have been offered a role in London."

"Yeah, I know, I'm really happy for you. I wish I had got the job I wanted on my first attempt." Rio hadn't gotten a role yet, so I could tell this may not have been a conversation he wanted to hear.

"Well, they have offered me the chance to work in the San Francisco office, which means I would be moving out to the US for the next eighteen months at least." *Kaiya, who knows what he is going to say, but remember it's okay no matter what. At least you're dealing with it now. Surely, he has to bring up the kiss now.*

"That's great you should take the job. San Francisco would be amazing. Don't get me wrong, working together in London would be amazing but I can't stop you from taking this journey, especially if it means earning less." *He has said working together would be amazing. But does he mean as friends or more? Then again, he doesn't want to stop me. Aww, he is so considerate. Or wait is that his way of telling me to go?*

"Seriously, you think I should take it?"

"Absolutely, it would be an opportunity like no other, and you enjoyed your time in the USA last year so much. I'm slightly jealous, I'd love to work there," Rio said, sipping his vodka coke.

"Well, I don't mind doing a different job if it means getting to spend some more time with my mum, Sarah and you. Also, there is something I need to tell you."

Kaiya you need to bring this up now. Otherwise, you're going to implode. Wait! What if he doesn't react in the right way? She will be fine. She has to do this, that way she knows she has tried. Take a deep breath. You cannot control his reaction Kaiya, just say what you need to.

"Kaiya, if it is serious can we talk about this another night as I want to just have fun and dance with you and everyone else." *Look, Kaiya he is avoiding it. Just do it. Go in. No! That's crazy, DO NOT DO THAT. Kaiya, look at how good he looks tonight. You know you want him to kiss you. Kaiya, tell him to kiss you!*

"Oh, Fuck it." I went in for the kiss. *This is actually happening. Go on, Kaiya! You actually did it. Yes, enjoy this. Be quiet, let me enjoy this. He is going to remember this. This was even better than the last time.* We pulled away from one another and just stared into one another's eyes. *He hasn't said anything. Why did you do that, Kaiya? Fuck, did I just screw up our friendship? That's it, I'm running to America; the decision is made. He hasn't said anything yet. Rio, come on! Hold on, Kaiya, look, he is getting closer to you. Wait a minute…*

He went in for another kiss. *See Kaiya, it was worth it. Wow, he is a good kisser. Now I see why El stayed with him for so long. If he kisses like this all the time, we are going to have so much fun. Kaiya is going to have her first boyfriend! Wait, don't say that. Lucia said not to get carried away. Kaiya, control yourself! Stop getting your expectations up. Just enjoy this!*

Rio had the biggest smile on his face, and so did I. We finally went back in, danced and enjoyed the night with the others. We didn't tell them what happened. At the end of the night, we had all booked a hotel to stay in but as I was sharing with the girls and Rio with the guys. We thought it would be best if nothing actually occurred.

Rio offered to drop me back home, so he and I were together on the M4 back to London from Bath. Rio was playing the album *These Things Happen* by G-Eazy – something we always played on long journeys when we wanted to relax or talk. I wasn't sure if last night was on his mind as he hadn't said anything about it for the first hour of the trip. *Should I bring it up again? I really wish more had happened. No, actually it's good it didn't. Time to bring this up, I'm not going to wait another fourteen months to talk about this one. I need to see where his head is at.*

"Kaiya, look about last night. I've wanted that kiss to happen for so long, but I don't think I am in the right headspace at the moment for anything to progress." *Stay calm, let's hear him out. Let's remind him that this wasn't our first kiss. But at least I know he has wanted it to happen. That's a good sign Kaiya.*

"Oh okay, you realise that wasn't our first kiss by the way," I said as I turned my body to face him.

"Huh? What do you mean?" *I know he likes to play jokes on me, but this is not the time to do so.*

"You don't remember the night out? That night during Easter last year?"

"Yeah, when we got obliterated, I have no memory of that night whatsoever." *Kaiya that is an insult on your kissing abilities, or was he actually that drunk? He can't be serious, can he?*

"Well I do, and we were making out in the smoker's area."

"Why didn't you bring this up before?" said Rio as he kept glancing over at me, whilst watching the road.

"Well neither did you," I said as I turned down the music until it was more background noise.

"I didn't know about it until now!"

"Seriously you had no memory whatsoever?" *Brilliant, I've had this going through my head for nearly fourteen months, and this idiot didn't have a clue as to what was going on. Are you joking! No Kaiya, this is not the time to lose your temper. Breathe. Breathe.*

"Does this look like the reaction of somebody who knew? And I just said to you I have wanted that kiss to happen for so long."

"Well, I didn't know you didn't know. I just thought you had avoided the whole situation, then you had that whole thing with Shreya too."

"Wait, how do you know about Shreya?" Rio said with a panicking undertone.

"You told me that night before we started making out."

Okay, let me be truthful. When he told me about Shreya, I was jealous. But I was also angry at her treatment of him, and also saw it as an opportunity to put our relationship into a new light.

"Okay, well I need a bit of time to process all of this, especially as you're also my best friend and I don't want to mess that up as well."

"But we both know we like each other." *Why does this have to be complicated? Rio just says yes, it's not that hard. No Kaiya, you cannot control him. Stop getting angry. Breathe.*

"I don't know if this is lust or something else."

"Oh…" *Brilliant. This boy is basically saying he just wants to fuck me. Then again, he is being honest with me. I can't fault him for that. Okay well, my heart just fell into my stomach.*

"Kaiya just give me some time please." The last twenty minutes of the journey was in silence. Rio dropped me off at my mum's house.

***

I'd moved in with Mum and Sarah after my final exams, and it was so much fun. But now a week had passed, and I hadn't heard anything from Rio. I messaged him, but he didn't respond. I only had a few days until my deadline, and I didn't know what to do. I headed out into town one day to clear my head. I always loved being in the centre of London and just people-watching with a coffee. It was my new way of clearing my thoughts. I began to change my perspective on things because I kept reminding myself that this was actually a really exciting time for me. If this had been me a year ago, I would have been the worst human being to be around probably for at least a week, and I would have taken it out on Mum. But I was changing, which was brilliant. As this voice in my head wouldn't shut up, I tried to close my eyes and breathe, but then I heard a voice yell my name.

"Kaiya, it that you?" I turned around, and as I did, I saw it was Asveekaar.

"Hi, Asveekaar." *I really can't deal with this girl right now. How was I friends with her for so long?*

"How's university been? Didn't Rio and Ashley go to Bath as well?"

"No, Ashley went to Bristol."

"Oh yeah, I presume you two are still together."

"Nope, we broke up a few years ago now."

"Oh well I did say same-sex relationships don't work, but you didn't want to listen." This is why I stopped being friends with her.

Kaiya Breathe, it's okay, let her say whatever she wants, it is up to you if you want to let it affect you.

"Look I actually need to go as I'm meant to be meeting someone," I said, walking off, while still facing her.

"Let me guess, it's Rio. Does he still have a crush on you?"

I stopped in my stride, maintaining my distance though. "Rio had a crush on me?" I wasn't sure if he did when I was at school, but it was nice to know that I was right about my hunch.

"Don't act like you didn't know. It was so obvious to us girls, and I'm pretty sure you liked him too."

"Well, Rio and I are not really speaking at the moment."

"Oh. Well, this is awkward then, isn't it? He always did have a way of being angry about everything. If I were you, it's probably for the best."

"He's changed a lot; he isn't the same person he used to be."

"Well sounds like you may be the one who likes him."

"Like I said, we aren't talking. Anyway, I've got to go. It's always a pleasure, Asveekaar," I said, moving on quickly and sarcastically.

I walked away satisfied because I hadn't let Asveekaar get to me like she used to at school. She hadn't changed as a person and was still horrible, which is why I didn't want to talk to her but was happy that I could deal with her now.

I called Rio that day and every day up until my deadline. I wanted to talk to him, but he didn't want to speak to me, and I had a decision to make. I knew I liked him, especially as I felt awful after the way our conversation ended, but Ahava and Lucia were right, I couldn't control everything. I had to start going with life's flow. Maybe this job was the right thing for me to do.

Learning to Observe

It had been nearly six months since I had left London for San Francisco. Working on myself and being submerged in that same type of atmosphere I'd experienced during my summer here was paying dividends. I was falling in love with working on my mental health and challenging myself. I kept up meditation, and it helped me to improve my own awareness. Living with my uncle and auntie was great, and I decided to push any thoughts of Rio out of my head.

Unfortunately, I couldn't sit in Lucia's office anymore, so we would Facetime instead. In my room, I had a big sofa and I always sprayed vanilla extract before a session and sat in the same position I used to adopt in her office – snuggled up with three pillows.

Rio and I hadn't spoken except on the odd few occasions over the last six months. He always messaged me on my dad's death anniversary and had a drink to honour his memory, but other than a bit of small talk we didn't really communicate. Thankfully I had Anisha and Amari, and our relationship only got better the longer I spent out there with them, but Rio had been integral to my life for the last five years, and I felt his loss deeply. I explained to Lucia that I realised I liked Rio far more than I'd ever thought but had to accept that he may or may not want me, and I wasn't sure if I was okay being just friends.

"Kaiya, I know you haven't wanted to talk about Rio, but I think now, after nearly six months, we should look at this." Even from across the ocean, she would hold me accountable to myself and my emotions.

"Okay, well I just push away any thoughts I have of him. I take a deep breath and disassociate from his memory."

"This does help remove the attachment, but is Rio somebody you want to lose as a friend after everything you two have been through?"

"Honestly, I don't want to lose him. More than anything, I am just trying to adapt to life and go with the flow. I don't want to try and control things, and for the first time when these thoughts about him reappear I remind myself of the present moment and that there is nothing I can do to change the past. I just wasn't sure how to handle reconnecting."

"Kaiya, do you think you ran away from it all, or did you actually want to be in San Francisco?"

"Honestly, at first, I wanted to run because of what had happened, but at the same time, I knew this could be a really exciting opportunity for me. It was definitely a combination of the two."

"Maybe you need to take some time to reflect on how you really feel. One way to check is to see what happens when you start thinking about the situation and how your body reacts. Then you'll know if you have moved on from it."

***

I thought long and hard about what Lucia had said. I gave myself a chance to really think and spent a few weeks trying to go deeper into my meditation. When thinking about Rio, my body would keep getting a gut-sinking feeling which meant no matter what I said to myself, I hadn't moved past it.

I loved being in the US, but I also missed home. I was really good friends with some of my co-workers, and one of them suggested a book for me because they knew I loved learning about mental health and understanding the thoughts that go through our heads. They recommended *The Untethered Soul* by Michael Singer, and it really helped me learn how to handle my emotions. The best thing I learnt from this book was to always remind myself that "I am the observer. I am not the emotion" and it allowed me to look at the crackhead as if it was separate to me and not actually me.

I would sit and think about the worst-case scenarios with Rio and see myself being okay and dealing with them. Lucia told me that if the worst-case scenario did occur, it would be hard for a while, but after everything I had been through, I'd be able to learn from it and conquer it.

After doing this for a few weeks, I was able to slowly let go of my emotions about Rio and not fight them. I began to feel comfortable in being okay with whatever was going to happen. More than anything, the stint I had done so far in the US was something I was so proud of.

However, it's weird how life works because it seemed that as soon as I fully accepted that Rio may not like me other than as a friend, or may not even want to be friends anymore, I saw an opportunity arise in the London office. It was to work on a really exciting project and something I knew I could add value to. The project was only for six months, but I knew I had to be on this team as soon as I saw the job post on our internal intranet. I spoke to my manager, and she helped me put in the transfer request as she saw how passionate I was, plus it would be really exciting to be back in London now with this newfound headspace I was in. I didn't tell anybody I was going back home, though.

My auntie and uncle were sad that I wasn't staying longer, but I knew I would be back again after six months. Whenever I thought of Rio saying, "No, let's just be friends" or "Sorry, Kaiya, I'm not sure I can be your friend anymore," it made me feel slightly upset but not distraught. I was just more excited about finally confronting the situation head-on. The bonds I'd forged with my cousins over the last six months were truly amazing, and I had more family than I realised. Looking back now, I knew that moving to San Francisco had been absolutely the right decision, and I had no regrets about it.

***

I arrived in the UK at the end of April. My project would end in October, just after Rio's twenty-fourth birthday but more importantly, my mum's fiftieth birthday in June that year. The day I got back, I asked Sarah to pick me up but not to tell my mum as I wanted to surprise her. The biggest aspect that came from being in the US was my new-found sense of self-belief in my ability to perform in the working world. I really thought I could do it now. I created a myriad of triggers, like having the contract as my screen saver to remind myself "I am capable" and that "I have proven it." Not only that, when I moved to the London office, they had also heard about the work I had done in the US over the last six months, and it was so nice to be appreciated. I was really excited to be back in London, but I had no idea what lay ahead for Rio or me. More than anything, I just wanted my friend back, and I was able to accept that he might not even want that. The more the crackhead spoke to me, the more I was able to realise that the crackhead was a separate entity. It wasn't me, and I could choose to be sucked into what it said, or I could ignore it. My crackhead had several personalities too, and, in many cases, there was more than one of them in my head at once. But everything that had happened over the last five years had led me to realise a few important things:

It's easier to walk and move to life's beat of the drum, rather than to try and control it.

When you're truly aligned with something, it will happen.

Don't ever rely on anyone to fill your cup.

Now that I have an awareness of my crackhead and some tools to deal with it, I cannot wait to see what life has in store for me. What adventures, what rollercoaster I will ride because I know I will be okay. For the first time in my life, I was now just moving with life's beat, and I was really enjoying it.

RIO ———————————————————————————

Time to Get Some Air

Before uni, I thought I was about to embark on a four-year journey of booze and debauchery. What a dickhead! I graduated in July, and I remember feeling unsatisfied when it all came to a close. After the first semester exams had finished, I thought I had done everything I needed to get a first. I strategised to ensure I balanced my coursework modules with my exam modules, I went to the gym, did meal prep every day for eight weeks and worked on my mental health every week with Kate (video sessions though as she was based in London). Above all, I maintained a work–life balance. Don't get me wrong, I worked hard when I needed to, but I also knew it was important not to burn out and take the mental breaks. Then our results were posted for the end of the first semester. *Are you taking the actual piss?! You know what, I don't care anymore.* That's how the crackhead responded after learning I'd only achieved a mid-level upper second. *Genuinely what was the point in doing everything if I was always going to fall short?*

This made me realise that I needed some time away from studying and a new challenge. I had always wanted to compete for the university, but never had the chance with golf, so I tried out for other random shit like gymnastics and trampolining. To my shock, I was invited to compete for Bath with the trampolining team at their final divisional competition. I had a choice, either get stuck back into work straight away or take a break. I needed a low first in my final semester, to get a first overall, or 43 per cent to get an upper second, so my buffer was in place. I wanted to make some memories and do something completely rogue that I had never done before, so I went for it.

Why did I try out for trampolining you may wonder? Honestly, they had good looking girls, and it was the closest

I'd get to Michael Jordan when he was soaring through the air. With that, I gave myself the name "Air Rio." (Yes, I got absolutely rinsed for that by Saint and Maaphee.) I spent the next four weeks practising four times a week, learning my routine, and then came the day of the competition.

The competition had six tiers depending on your skill level, with one being the best and six being the worst. I was competing in tier six. With eighteen people competing in my division, I was nervous but also excited. I had that full competitive setting I had always wanted. Walk in, see the competition, feel the nerves. Breathe. Focus. Execute. I loved it. Our routine had ten tricks, and on every single bounce, you had to execute your move. You couldn't take an extra jump in between or your routine was over. We had to do the routine twice, and all I wanted to do was get through both routines in full succession.

In the end, I narrowly missed getting third place, but I was ecstatic having only stepped foot onto a trampoline for the first time four weeks before. I'd also made new friends and new memories which were exactly what my brain needed because once the tournament was over, I was able to relight that fire in my belly. It was all hands-on deck for the final exam season, and I was going to give it my everything. That way, I could walk away saying no matter what, I couldn't have done any more. I knew that grades didn't matter for getting a job, but for me, this was just something I wanted to prove to myself.

In early July, our results arrived, and three of my favourite modules which I had taught the entire syllabus to eight of my friends were my worst three marks. All the people I taught got higher than I did. I didn't have a scooby[25] as to how that happened. After these results came out, I had to really let go of my university experience and fully accept everything that had happened. No matter what I thought, I couldn't change anything now.

---

25 I didn't have a scooby = I didn't have a clue (Cockney rhyming slang).

I arrived at university with the expectations of having a girlfriend when I left, getting a first, securing a graduate role and having a six-pack. I didn't achieve any of my goals. Zero. I had to close the mental account of expectations that I'd created when I was thirteen. These "must-dos" had been sitting on my shoulders for just under a decade, and I felt like I had nothing to show for it. I did everything I physically could, and nothing worked, yet when I'd applied this strategy during placement year, it had worked. I was able to deliver a presentation to my entire division based on a project I had been working on for six months in the final few days before I left.

Thankfully Kate explained the following to me: "Anything with emotional investment creates hope, attachment and perceived gains. When you don't achieve those goals, your brain considers this a loss. Your mind perceives it, in the same way, a death. You placed all those expectations on something, and now they haven't happened, that means you're going to go through mourning."

Knowing this, meant I accepted that I was going to be upset for a while, and I was okay with it. I didn't beat myself up, and the crackhead didn't either.

Kate also told me, "This can happen in any stage of life. When expectations are not met, the level of emotional investment attached to them is only known by you, therefore don't be discouraged if anybody tells you to get over this quickly. Only you invested the emotions, therefore only you will know how much this has impacted you." There was no point in fighting it. I just had to give it time.

This Is Not a Drill

Graduation had occurred the day before and tonight was the big night – Grad Ball. This was the party to close out the last four years of hard work. Now was the time to relax and celebrate all the memories, friendships and everything I had learnt. University was over, and every time I was asked that question, "How do you feel now that university has ended?" I would always feel a kick in my gut. But I was also so relieved, knowing I never had to study again. I was ready for the real world. Kaiya was wearing a red full-length dress, but it didn't cover her left leg. She looked unreal. The two of us were outside sitting together when she brought up her new role.

"Rio, so you know that I have been offered a role to work in London?"

I told her I was happy for her. I hadn't secured anything, which meant that I had to work out what I was going to do for a year. I was going to be reapplying in September for the following year, but I had no idea how to keep myself busy till then.

"Well, they have offered me the chance to work in the San Francisco office, which means I would be moving to the US for the next eighteen months at least."

My heart sunk, but I knew I couldn't stop her from going because this was such an amazing opportunity. You want her to stay, but what kind of a friend says that, let alone someone who may like her more. Actually, Rio, tell her to stay. No, no, no, what am I thinking, tell her to go, don't be an idiot.

"That's great you should take the job. San Francisco will be amazing. Don't get me wrong, working together in London would be amazing too but I can't stop you from taking this journey."

"Seriously, you think I should take it?"

"Absolutely, it would be an opportunity like no other."

"Well I can do the same job here in London, it's just a different city. Rio, also there is something I need to tell you." *Does she want to stay or not? Why are girls so confusing?*

Just tell me straight. Forget this, I want to just enjoy myself tonight. I want happy memories of this night, not to look back and remember this.

"Kaiya, if it is serious can we talk about this another night as I want to just have fun and dance with you and everyone else."

"Oh Fuck it," Kaiya said as she leaned in and kissed me.

I thought I was dreaming. Wait, what if Kaiya wants to have sex? Oh shit, here we go. Does she like me? If this is going to happen, I need to be able to perform tonight. For fuck sake, how has all of this just gotten into my head? Take a breath, Rio, get your shit together. Shit, she is staring at me, kiss her again, Rio!

I went in again. I was on cloud nine. This felt so right. *I need to be on my game tonight. Okay, what do I remember from all the porn I have watched? I really want to kiss her more. Shit, I think I do like her. Or is this just all my emotions talking. Fuck, I can't mess this up with her.*

Kaiya had the biggest smile on her face, and so did I. We finally went back in, danced and enjoyed the night with the others. We didn't tell them what happened. At the end of the night, we had all booked a hotel, but as I was sharing with the guys and Kaiya with the girls, we thought it would be best if nothing actually occurred. I gave a sigh of relief, but also, I really wanted it to happen.

On the journey back to London, Kaiya and I didn't really talk about the kiss. I wanted to take her right there and then, the minute she kissed me, but I still had some nerves to deal with, and my head wasn't in the right place after all the expectations I'd had to deal with. Although I thought before we got back, something needed to be said.

"Kaiya, look about last night. I've wanted that kiss to happen for so long, but I don't think I am in the right headspace at the moment for anything to progress."

"Oh okay, you realise that wasn't our first kiss by the way."

"Huh? What do you mean?" *I thought she was chatting shit at this point. How the hell do you forget the first kiss with this girl of all people? She had to be lying.*

142

"You don't remember the night out? That night in Easter last year."

"Yeah, when we got obliterated, I have no memory of that night whatsoever."

"Well I do, and we were making out in the smoker's area."

Fuck, she's serious. How can I not remember any of this? Oh my God, that is why the dreams of her have felt so real!

"Why didn't you bring this up before?"

"Well, neither did you."

"I didn't know about it until now!"

"Seriously, you had no memory?"

"Does this look like the reaction of somebody who knew that? And I just said to you I have wanted that kiss to happen for so long."

"Well, I didn't know you didn't know. I just thought you had avoided the whole situation, then you had that whole thing with Shreya too."

GHADHERO![26] I'd told her about Shreya. Idiot!

"Wait, how do you know about Shreya?'

"You told me that night before we started making out." *Wait… so telling her made her want to kiss me? Shit, she got a bit jealous.*

"Okay, well I need a bit of time to process all of this, especially as you're also my best friend and I don't want to mess that up as well."

"But we both know we like each other." *She's right. But why am I confused then?*

"I don't know if this is lust or something else." *Oh, Rio, why did you just say that? Idiot, idiot, idiot. You like this girl. Or do you? How do you not know what you want?*

"Oh…"

"Kaiya, just give me some time, please."

I dropped Kaiya off at her mum's house, and we didn't speak for a month or so after this. This had really created a divide in

---

26 Ghadhero = Donkey (Gujarati)

our relationship. I wasn't scared and to be honest I craved this, but it is also why I didn't want to jump in. I couldn't screw this one up, and more importantly, I had to fix my shit before I could start anything with Kaiya.

***

September arrived, and Kaiya reached out to me. She had accepted the job in San Francisco. On her final day here, I went and said goodbye to her, but it wasn't like old times. This was different. I had really fucked this one up.

4-aco

The day I did magic mushrooms, or as the illegal substance aficionados would call it, 4-aco was one of my most insightful days.

Saint had tried all this stuff before and told me it wouldn't make me nauseous like magic mushrooms (4-aco was like a synthetic mushroom pill) but gives the same introspective and creative trip. I had been curious about psychedelics for a while, but Saint always kept telling me of his friend who used them as a way to run away from life instead of dealing with it. He didn't want the same thing to happen to me. He knew a lot had been happening in my life, so I'm glad he told me about this as it allowed me to fully get into a headspace where I knew this would be a one-time trip and I was going to get the best out of it. The psychodynamic therapy had helped me understand a lot of my root problems which allowed me get to a place in my life where I was feeling so self-assured and calm. I had been doing extensive research on the use of psychedelics to ensure, that if anything did go wrong, I had the tools around me to help bring myself back. I had created a list of my intentions for the trip, which included being creative and also to learn more about myself. This allowed my subconscious to focus on these points and I am so glad I did all of this preparation beforehand. I knew no matter what was happening, I would always face it head-on, and I was no longer running from my problems. In other words, I was ready. This only enhanced my trip down the yellow brick road, and it was amazing.

***

Lying under a tree with my cousin Ria as my safety net, I embarked on my journey down the rabbit hole. (She was a bit of nutcase herself and had tried shit like this before back in Rio De Janeiro, so she knew what to expect, but anyway that's enough about her, back to me.)

We had a piercing blue sky that would have made the clearest oceans jealous. Combined with the music we were playing, every song was like a music video. The fast pace of drum and bass of "Parallel" by Technimatic began my journey by swinging on a cloud that was actually a pirate ship with all the crew and the captain as my internal crackheads.

"Blueberry Faygo" by Lil Mosey took me to a tropical beach where all my crackheads were surfing, dancing as hula girls or making sand angels in the sun.

"Natural Blues" by Moby intensified the trip by creating fractal patterns that streaked off into blades of light that transformed into a gigantic lighting version of me in the middle of space as I watched on. My neocortex (the part of the brain that controls imagination) was smashing memories, dreams and whatever I could see in front me together to create worlds and ideas I had never seen before. But it wasn't until I decided to meditate while listening to "Bamboo" by Elder Island that my trip transformed.

Not only did I have a wicked trip...

I returned feeling like everything in life was going to be alright

Life Knocks When You're Ready for It

Kaiya leaving gave me a lot on which to reflect. I started feeling sad, mostly about her but also about my expectations essentially dying. My twenty-third birthday arrived in October, and after only receiving messages through texts, I realised the impact social media was having on my life. It reminded me of women, jobs, how successful other people are and their amazing physiques. So, I cut it all off. I went cold turkey instantly. Facebook, Instagram and Snapchat. I also learnt how to start state shifting using music. This was one of the best tools in my arsenal. On top of this, I took a meditation course which helped improve my practice, and I became committed to doing it daily. No matter what, I made sure to get in one if not two sessions and it immediately started making me feel better. The combination of no social media and meditating every day allowed me to learn how to control the crackhead.

***

After three months of meditating every single day and logging my practice on a calendar to remind me how much I had invested and how far I'd come – it also stopped me looking for short-term gratifications.

I had been thinking in such a positive way, manifesting what I wanted and got to the final stages of assessment centres and interviews for companies I really wanted to be in. I was in such a good place, and I genuinely believed I had started learning how to control the crackhead. Then life decided to give me a test, and within three weeks, all of the roles got filled by other people. It was body blow after body blow. The worst was Fuji, a smaller design company. Saint and I had applied together, and he had managed to get in, but I didn't. I remember crying the day I got the email. This felt worse than ending the relationship with El. My expectations had gotten the better of me through trying to manifest. I kept thinking of only positive outcomes, getting excited about life and what I was going to do. I kept thinking about how I would feel when Fuji called to offer me the job, but that never came.

Before this, Kate and I had been having sessions where I was positive about life. We were talking about all the good that had happened in the last three months. I never knew you could use therapy as a way to also reflect on all the good you've had going on too. It really allowed me to feel grateful for everything that was happening, so when all these body blows occurred, it was shit. Again, Kate was a saving grace during this period as all it took was a perspective change. I really thought I had found my formula.

"Rio, it's okay to mourn this, take the time you need and let the emotions go through you," Kate said.

"I did everything I was supposed to. I did it all right. I thought positively. I did everything I had to. What more does this planet want from me? Honestly just let something go my way for once please." I didn't feel angry, I just felt done. Done with it all. Done with life. This was a worse feeling than after graduation.

"Rio, part of the process is that you say you kept thinking positive thoughts and imagining all the good, but it also creates a form of expectation. It's another grieving period again now for you, but it's okay. Keep giving yourself the self-love. Since you gave up social media, this is the first session where I couldn't hear the smile in your voice in the last three months."

"So how do I manifest or think of the future without having expectations. All of these books, spiritual texts say to use this. Also, CEOs look and visualise as part of their success strategies. What do I do then?"

"Look just because what you want doesn't come to you now doesn't mean it won't necessarily happen. Do all of this, keep this thinking process as it's such an asset but with one tweak. Don't put a time frame on it and once you have envisioned it, let it go. Understand and accept that what is meant to be for you will be for you and move with life's flow."

After letting that session sink in, I started to feel better about life again. It took time, but something really strange also happened to me. I went for a long drive to clear my head, and I remember asking the question out loud, "If I am on the right track, please show me a butterfly." I carried on driving and forgot about the question. Three days later, I was walking down New Bond Street with my cousins in the evening. We walked past a building which had some lights being projected on to it. We couldn't work out what it was until one of my cousins said, "I think it's a butterfly." Then we realised a butterfly the size of the building was being projected on to it, with hundreds of little butterflies around it. But me being me, I thought, "Oh that's quite cool," not remembering what I had asked beforehand.

Only when I got home and started speaking to my dad did I have my lightbulb moment. In an instant, I felt this sensation of relief. *Everything was going to be alright,* and I had faith that it would be. Now I knew something was changing. I started reading the book *The Surrender Experiment* by Michael Singer. This book changed the way I was thinking on a profound level. My new motto for life became "Stop fighting life. Surrender and move with it."

What a difference this has made. In that time, I've been able to remove all my expectations. I've reached a milestone of consecutively meditating and not being on social media for over eight months. I was never going to go back to how I used to think. I started surrendering to life when I didn't want to and began to have small but highly euphoric moments in such simple things like seeing that the sun was shining today instead of it raining. I realised that all of this was to build the mental toolset I needed, because after this happened Puma decided to reject me going back as a graduate. I accepted this, and I was able to fully close that chapter. What I didn't expect was that they would call me ten days later and offer me a role back that they thought I was perfect for because of the way I carried myself during my placement year.

I was finally in a place where I was happy being on my own, content with my own thoughts, and then life knocked and offered me a graduate role. I realised the more control I kept trying to have over life the unhappier I was because what I wanted to be wasn't necessarily what life had in store for me. I couldn't change what it would do so I started to surrender and move with it.

I was now able to reflect on my kiss with Kaiya in a way that allowed me to truly understand what was going on in my head. I started panicking about relationships because it created anxiety. However, after maintaining months of meditation – as well as no social media, reading this new book, giving up porn and no masturbation – I got to a point where the thought of sex didn't make me feel like I wasn't good enough. When I realised I had awoken to this new state I knew I was finally content in my own skin. I had been training, and I was in the best shape of my life, which made me feel even better.

What reaffirmed this was that I ended up having a one-night stand after a night out with some friends. I wasn't panicked or anxious, and I was just enjoying myself the way I used to. What was more amazing, was the crackhead was also quieter. I couldn't believe it. I was ready for the next phase of life, especially before my graduate role began, and I was excited to see where it would lead.

Kaiya and I had spoken briefly while she was in the US but not much. I missed her like crazy though as I was becoming more in tune with my new mindset. I realised that actually, we would be really good together, but I also had to become content in knowing she may have found someone else. I was ready to reconnect with her properly, and it is so funny how life works because a few days after accepting all of this, there was a knock on the door.

"Hey, Rio."

"Kaiya…"

Oh shit, here we go…

The End

PART II

Before we Continue...

STOP! BEFORE YOU CONTINUE, I RECOMMEND GETTING A JOURNAL/PIECE OF PAPER AND PEN.

This part of the book will dive into real life practices, look at the psychology as well as the spiritual aspects of different neural patterns and habits. I have personally used all of these to help me on my journey and I will be providing you with as many tips and tricks I have learnt along the way as well as where I have learnt them from. Some exercises may work for you, others may not, hopefully there will be something you will be able to take away from this section.

I have included a challenge at the end of this section called "The 50-Day Crackhead Challenge" or 50CC for short.

— 1 —

Understanding Your Crackhead

In the preface, I described how your behaviour is a culmination of all your habits, actions, beliefs, energy, thoughts and emotions, and that dictates your reality. The more you think in a certain way, the more it becomes your "norm."

Through nearly five years of therapy, reading several different books and trying out different techniques, I have learnt that the real battle is dealing with the crackhead inside us. Some of the best books I have read regarding this topic were the two written by Michael Singer *(The Surrender Experiment and The Untethered Soul).*

I like using the term crackhead, as the shock factor of the words helps creates the idea of this thing/voice in your head as being crazy but also a cartoon. You have seen some of the thoughts going through Kaiya's and Rio's heads but here are a few more examples I have collected from people:

- *I'm insecure, what will he think? Do I come off too silly? Am I too fussy or irrational? Am I good enough for him? Is she more his type?*

- *Does she like my physique? If I'm with her, does that mean I will have to be like my dad? I don't want to have to depend on her. Let me run from this. But I want to be in a relationship. Or do I? I don't want to get hurt, but I want to have fun. Nope, this is too much.*

- *I've seen bad relationships in the family. I have to be independent. I need my space. What are they going to expect from me? Why am I freaking out this is only a first date!*

- *Is he just trying to get into my pants? Does he like me for me? Maybe he likes certain parts. I don't know. That's it I'm not going to put out. Actually, fuck him. Then again, do I want to fuck him? Maybe I could play him at his own game. Should I ask him to pay for stuff? Don't be like that. You know what let's just leave this whole thing entirely.*

The voice in our head is crazy because it constantly changes its mind about a situation. Similarly, it also creates fictitious perspectives of scenarios that may never happen, which then makes us anxious and or upset. Now that you are aware of the crackhead write down every thought you have, or just listen to them and have a look at what they are saying.

To paraphrase Michael Singer, spend one entire day with your person (crackhead) after seeing how often they change their mind, how conflicted or emotionally overreactive they can be, why would you ever ask them for advice about relationships or your finances?[27]

This crackhead creates emotions in us that we often don't enjoy. Remember this emotion is only affecting you because of the way you have been brought up – your conditioning. Your emotions are based on your likes and dislikes, all of which come from the environmental factors and the way of living you have become accustomed to. If you were born in another part of the world, your entire life would be different. What you like and dislike would change. Therefore, the only constant thing is you. You. Not your emotions.

You cannot get rid of this crackhead. They will always be there. All you can do is decide how much you let it affect

---

27 Singer, M. (2007). *The Untethered Soul.* (Yellow Kite Books); pp15–22.

you. You have to be committed to working on your own self-awareness, and the following exercises can help you do that. The more you can disassociate your thoughts and find self-awareness, the easier it becomes to stay in the state of calmness and to ebb and flow with life. Your ability to be the observer becomes stronger and stronger.

Self-acceptance

Accepting who you are is one of the most fundamental ways of dealing with deep-rooted emotions. Self-acceptance and self-love are so important in our mental health and how we perceive the world. The amount of change you could create in yourself in a short space of time is phenomenal if you begin to really start accepting the past and not fight it.

Practice: Self-acceptance

1. Begin by writing down some of the fears and/or parts about yourself that you cannot accept. Include any limiting beliefs you have created too.

2. Ask yourself when these thoughts started. (It is okay if you don't know in this moment – now that you have asked yourself the question your subconscious will start working on it.) Just a rough age when you first remember having each of these thoughts.

3. Now consider if this is something you created in your own head or is it something that has actually happened to you. You may be surprised to see how many thoughts and limiting beliefs you have created through fictitious scenarios in your head that are not real, but may stem from only one thing

that actually occurred in your life. I was shocked myself when I realised the number of limiting beliefs I had created as the by-product of only one event. I now realise my crackhead had replayed that event over and over again that it all felt very real.

4. Now if the event actually happened to you, the first step is to accept that it has happened. No matter how much time you spend thinking about it, it will *never ever change*. Let me emphasise that again. No matter how much you think about it, it is solidified in the past and will *never ever change*. So, don't waste your energy looking back but use that energy to look at the here and now. Take a moment to think of this event, visualise it and take some deep breaths. Allow the emotions to overcome you and visualise them entering your body and then passing through the back of you.

5. Every time the thought comes into your head, say this out loud, "I accept this thought for what it is, and I let it pass. I control how I feel, and I feel good." This is something I say to myself over and over again.

Now, this is important. Things like this take time. **It is not a quick fix.** You are trying to rewire connections in your brain that have been there for several years and are so strong right now. Think of this as breaking a habit. Instead of it being a physical habit, it's a neural habit, but it is one that can be changed, it just depends on how much you want to change it. Next look at the language you use.

Changing Your Language

The words we use have an effect on who we are. If we continuously use language that is bad for our psyche, then over time it begins to embed within us. We begin to start thinking in certain patterns and ways. As these thought patterns grow stronger, they slowly become habitual. In the same way, we have habits, we also have thinking habits. To change from a negative thinker to a positive one, we have to begin by changing thinking patterns which stem from the words we use. The brain is lazy and therefore uses the strongest synapses first over the weaker ones, which is why once you have formed a habit initially it is difficult to break it, but as the new behaviour imbeds over time those connections grow in strength and become your "norm." Remember thinking in a certain way is like any muscle. The more you practise the stronger you'll become.

The thought and the vocalised word of the human race carries its own vibration. When we speak, we create sound. Sound has its own atomic structure and therefore its own vibrational frequency (the rate at which the atoms will vibrate). Dr Masaru Emoto did an experiment on the effect words have on the crystal patterns formed when water turns to ice. His results found that positive words such as love, gratitude, eternal, peace all created intricate and highly detailed crystal patterns, whereas phrases such as evil, you disgust me, fool all created distorted and "unappealing" patterns and shapes.[28] What does this tell you? Words have their own vibration which has an impact on water, and given that our body is 60–70 per cent water, how do you think the words you not only think but say out loud will have an impact on who you are as a person? This reiterates one of Confucius's famous quotes "He who says he can and he who says he can't are both usually right."

Marissa Peers was named Britain's best therapist by *Men's* Health *Magazine*,[29] and her videos have been truly transformational

28 https://thewellnessenterprise.com/emoto/
29 May 2006: https://peoplepill.com/people/marisa-peer/

for me.[30] She has a course called the "Uncompromised Life", which you can access through Mindvalley[31] (an online learning platform) and was something that helped me on my journey. I'd recommend checking out both Marissa and Mindvalley.

One way I was able to change my language was by writing it down and creating triggers for myself. Triggers are so important because when our brain becomes tired, or we feel emotionally low, the triggers can help boost us when we need them. Here's how to do it:

Practice: Changing Your Words

This exercise is in two parts:

1. Part 1: For 30 days, write down in a journal what you are most happy about with yourself. It can be anything like "I am proud of myself for starting this journey," "I love my enthusiasm for work," etc. Make an effort to recognise something about yourself that you are happy about and applaud it. This is how you start to build your internal reservoir.

2. Part 2: Next write down one piece of negative language you use, for example, I'm overweight because I have a slow metabolism, I hate running, and so on. Next, write the opposite of it, for example, my metabolism is so fast, I love running, and so on.
   a. A negative piece of language I used to use was I have to be rich and successful for a beautiful girl to love me. I changed this to I attract not only beautiful women into my life but those that are right for me. They will love me for me, not my success.

---

30 https://www.youtube.com/watch?v=xSUfLyrhJME
31 See Resources, page 195, for Mindvalley website.

3. **EXTRA:** I recorded myself saying all of my positive affirmations. I would play it before bed and in the morning when I would be the most receptive to new information. Close your eyes as you listen to it and envision yourself with all of these attributes. The more you start believing in yourself, the more you'll start behaving in that way and making real changes to your life, so that you constantly feel like this. (Below are examples of some of my affirmations.)

   a. For self-confidence: I love my self-confidence. People recognise my confidence. I am a magnet and people enjoy spending time with me.

   b. For body image: I have my best body. I have such a fast metabolism. I can build muscle and lose fat whenever I choose to.

   c. For improved outlook: I am so grateful for my family, friends, the people who care about me. I am so happy that I look after my own happiness.

Here are two stories I would like to share. One about myself and one of my friend, let's call her Jane

Jane used to say "I am the disappointment in the family" as a joke, but it secretly ate away at her for years. She always compared herself to her elder sister and would make this remark in front of her parents and friends too. Her parents never thought this and told her to stop saying it, but she didn't listen. She thought humour would help her own this limiting belief. In the last year, she has finally stopped saying it and her self-confidence has grown enormously. She changed it to "I am somebody that I would be proud off" and honestly the person she is today after ten months is completely different to the girl I knew for many years. She's the happiest I have ever seen her, and she has managed to get a job she loves as a pastry chef. **Don't give yourself any reason to stop believing in yourself especially if you know you are prone to falling back into that negative thinking pattern.**

I have never enjoyed doing cardio, but every time I feel like I don't want to do it, I remind myself of how much I love to run. I keep saying it as I'm doing it. Then I try and make myself laugh as well. When your brain is laughing, you're in a state of joy, and you anchor the emotion of joy with the activities you're doing, which in this case is running. Now I genuinely enjoy running, and I have fun when doing it. (This was one of the methods that helped me lose weight and then attempt *Insanity Asylum*, a forty-minute cardio-based workout, which I managed to complete. I used this technique through every exercise session.)

The more you use this reframing practice, the more your neural pathways will start to branch out and create new thought patterns and habits. Eventually, you'll be able to train yourself so that your natural habitual state is to constantly remind yourself of how good life is for you and that will eventually shift your state of mind.

Meditation

Meditation is arguably one of the best tools in my toolbox. Establishing a regular practice can help remove anxiety, fear, sadness, etc. Ideally, you need to practise in the morning for about twenty minutes, but if you're in a rush, do ten. After the first eight months of daily practice, I now meditate before lunch as opposed to the mornings. I found it brings me back down to neutral as my morning workload is quite extensive – some people prefer to do a morning and an afternoon practice. Do whatever works for you but always do your practise before eating and caffeine because you're trying to slow and calm your body down, not stimulate it.

Practice: Meditation

There are several guided meditation apps, YouTube clips you can watch, but the following practice can also help build mental concentration and focus as another by-product. I have used Headspace (have a look at the Netflix special it's great), Beeja and lots of other YouTube clips, but the following practice is the one that has helped me the most.

1. Find a comfortable position to sit in. You may choose to use the lotus position, half-lotus or any traditional form, use a meditation cushion/stool or just sit on a chair. Just make sure your back is straight.

2. Close your eyes and imagine floating above the world in whichever position you are sitting in (on a chair, lotus position, etc.). This helps put your size and anything you may be going through into perspective compared to the size of the earth, and even the universe.

3. Next, imagine tree roots, anchors, lighting bolts, whatever you decide coming from the bottom of your feet into the earth. (If you're sitting in the lotus position imagine it is coming from the part of your knees which are touching the floor.)

4. Next, imagine tree roots, anchors, lighting bolts, whatever you decide, coming from the bottom of your spine.

5. Take a deep breath in and exhale. Repeat this ten times, drawing in as much oxygen as you can. Feel the blood going through your body. Feel your hands, your legs, your heart beating and become present in this moment.

6. Start your timer for the length of time you want to meditate.

7. The "Three Pillars of Zen" talks about using the mantra *Mu* (think of the noise a cow makes, but not as aggressive; the "u" is pronounced the same as the "u" in the word "put"). Begin by saying this. Keep your focus on the mantra. Say it in your head. If you drift off into other thoughts, it is okay, just bring your attention back to the mantra and continue. Your aim is to be like water, flow and bend, don't be rigid and structured. As you practise, your attention will get better and better.

8. If you prefer not to use a mantra, count the breaths you take. On every exhale count one, then two, then three and so on until you get to the number ten. Once you have hit ten, start counting backwards until you get to one. Repeat the process. If your mind drifts or you forget your position, simply return back to the number one and continue.

9. You may like to create your own mantra: e.g., "I have an abundance of success, love, creativity, sex and financial wealth in my life and inspire those around me to attract the same." You can also use the word "Aum" (think Hinduism here) or any word you resonate with.

10. Once the timer has gone off, I would recommend just sitting there and relaxing with your own thoughts for a few (I like to do three) minutes. Think of your brain as a computer that has just written new software. These final three minutes allow the software to download into your body. In these three minutes, you do not need to say the mantra or count. Just simply be there with your thoughts

— 2 —

Living with a crackhead

Asthmatics usually have two inhalers – one brown and one blue. The brown is a preventative measure, to be taken regularly and the blue is used in times of distress for instant relief. Think of the previous section as the brown inhaler. Regular practice will lead to long-term effects that change who you are and reduce your overall symptoms. But what happens when life throws a curveball at you, and you need some instant relief? How do you calm the crackhead before they go on an all-out assault? Something I call state shifting has always helped me do this.

State Shifting

We all have times, despite practising positive thinking, that we feel at the mercy of our crackhead. No matter what we do, we cannot get out of the state. NLP (Neuro-Linguistic Programming) talks about anchoring emotions to different objects or sounds. As you now know words have an impact on water and therefore you, and so does music. I used music to "State Shift."

Practice: Changing States

This following practice offers you a fast way of changing your mindset simply by listening to some music. The interesting thing about this practice is that it shows how easy it is to shift states.

1. Begin by finding a song or album you love. The more songs you can find, the better, as you'll get bored of some songs one day and want to hear others. Other times you may need to listen to more than one song to boost your mood.

2. Put the song on and start singing to it.

3. Dance to it. When your body is moving, it helps create endorphins (happy hormones) to change your state.

4. Make sure you are smiling and laughing.

5. Force a smile if you have to and start making yourself laugh. The more you get involved in this emotion, the stronger it will register with this song. Sing at the top of your lungs if you have to.

6. Continue dancing and singing until you feel your mood start to improve.

7. Once the song has ended, make sure you make this song sacred. This is now your "trigger song." If you feel sad and you play the song, you have to go through all of those emotions again. Sing, dance, smile, laugh etc. You're reinforcing every time you hear this song that you can change the way you feel in an instant. You control your thoughts. Remember, you are the observer, not the emotion. If you find yourself playing the song and you cannot get into it, then stop the song and play something else. Try again at another point. Use another song.

D.U.E.

If you are not able to perform state shifting, for example because you are at work, then try this exercise which can be done while you sit at your desk and is something I call "Dissolving Unwanted Emotions". Use this technique whenever you have feelings or memories you want to remove yourself from. This was a quick way I was able to bring myself back to equilibrium when I would get tangled in a web of my own thoughts.

Practice: D.U.E.

1. Part of this exercise is to imagine yourself coming out of your body so that you can witness your own story, meaning you can see as a third person the events unfold in front of you which negatively impacted you. Watch this clip from the film *Doctor Strange* if you find it difficult to visualise: https://www.youtube.com/watch?v=wReny0b3_ds. Watch from 1.56 minutes to 2.03 minutes.

2. The next time a negative thought goes through your head, first take a deep breath.

3. Next pause the thought, the same way you would pause a film.

4. Now imagine your ghost version coming out of your body (the same way *Doctor Strange* did), so now you are looking at the scene from the third person. You can still see your body that is going through the negative experience, but the scene is paused.

5. Next, imagine that scene dissolving into a black screen (as if looking at a TV switched off), once you have that in your mind just hold that moment of seeing nothing and feeling nothing for a few seconds.

6. Finish by taking three big deep breaths in and out, open your eyes and come back to the present. Hopefully you will feel more relaxed and able to continue.

— 3 —

Bringing the Crackhead Down in Size

The exercises in the last two chapters are long- and short-term measures that can help you overcome your symptoms, but the crackhead will never truly go away unless you deal with the root cause of your problems. Remember the crackhead feasts on insecurities, expectations, memories, anything it can get its hands on from the past.

Psychodynamic therapy (when you look back at your past to understand what has caused certain personality traits and feelings) with CBT (Cognitive Behavioural Therapy – creating coping mechanisms or "tools" to be able to deal with your crackhead) has been the biggest learning lesson of my life.

When I first began therapy, my parents and friends didn't know, and when I told them I was attending regular sessions, they immediately thought the worst. I decided to go to therapy because I wanted to learn more about myself, discuss my thoughts openly and freely, but the most important reason was to gain an unbiased opinion on my situation. Those closest to you are naturally biased, but a therapist looks in an unbiased, neutral position. When I explained to them that this is the reason I sought out therapy, their perception changed instantly. Your car needs regular servicing and you see a doctor for your physical health so why would you not carry out regular checks on your mental health?

Everything I've shared with you so far in Part II is to help you become more mindful and self-aware. By becoming more self-aware, we also become present in the moment, i.e., learning what a "good" and "bad" emotion is as it is happening as opposed to after the event is over.

As the crackhead speaks, you learn to become an observer to them. You don't react to the "good" or "bad." You learn to just watch the emotions go through you and not attach to it. Your next question though maybe, "I want to hold onto the good emotions, surely that can't be a bad thing. Why should I just watch them?"

Well, that is your choice.

Being the Observer

By being the observer, we realise we don't have to get caught up unnecessarily unless we choose to while remembering that each state of "happiness" and "sadness" is only momentary. These moments can add up into, days, weeks, months or years, but eventually the sad times will pass and so will the good; it's about learning not to hold onto them. Holding on to good emotions is as unhealthy as holding onto bad emotions. By understanding that the "good" is only temporary helps us appreciate the moment far more when we're experiencing it. Then let it go through us rather than trying to trap it inside us forever.

If you can let the "good" go through you, you are also able to let the "bad" go through you as well. This doesn't mean you forget the good or the bad. You become fully appreciative as the moment occurs, enjoy it as much as you can and then once it is over you go back to neutral as opposed to being sad that it is over.

The way I have learnt to remember "I am the observer and not the emotion" is through the following visualisation process, which you may find helpful.

Practice: Being the Observer

This exercise is a great way to recentre yourself and let go of what has happened in the past.

1. Close your eyes and, just as in the meditation practice I shared in the previous chapter, begin by imagining that you are sitting in a chair floating above the Earth. Look down and remind yourself of how small you are compared to the Earth. Now look in front of you and understand how small you are compared with the universe. This is not to say that you are inconsequential, but to remind you that everything is connected. We are a part of the universe, the earth, and that the fact we can live and breathe on this earth is an absolute phenomenon.

2. Now in front of you is a cloud of different energies with different colours. This cloud of energy is your emotions. Imagine green going through for your likes, red for dislikes, whatever it maybe there is a colourful swirling cloud of energies in front you.

3. Every time you let your emotions get the better of you, you are not sitting in your chair, you are currently standing in the cloud of energies. Your emotion has sucked you in, and now you're too close to it to be able to look at it objectively.

4. When you realise you are no longer sitting down, take five big deep breaths in and out. Allow yourself to sit back down in the chair.

5. Once you are sitting down, realise that this emotion has somewhat affected you but DON'T FIGHT IT. If somebody has annoyed you, made you upset, no matter what the feeling is, do not fight it. By thinking I should ignore this, or trying to forget it or push it away, you are reinforcing that it has affected you. You are giving that emotion more strength. Instead, imagine yourself sitting in that chair again.

6. Now associate a colour with that emotion.

7. Next imagine a lightning bolt in that colour going through your body, through your heart and then leaving your body. It has created a hole, and it is powering through now.

8. Think of the event in your head and say in your head "I am accepting what has happened. I am the observer. The emotion passes through me."

9. Keep breathing through it. Take big deep breaths in and out as you imagine all of this. As you do this, you will slowly start to reduce how you feel.

10. When you feel it is right, imagine the lightning bolt stopping and your body repairing the hole that is created. You notice there is no scar. Your body is healthier and better than it was before because you have just learnt how to deal with your emotions and be the observer.

11. Open your eyes, smile, listen to some good music and enjoy your day.

Soon you'll get to a point where you may not need to do the second part of the exercise as you can maintain your seat in the observer chair. Remember that this is eventually meant to become a state of mind as it means that moving forward you are able to stay clear and calm through whatever it is life decides to test you with.

— 4 —

Expectations, Relationships and Avoidance

Relationships are what make life great. The connections we build with people create our environment and lead us down paths we may not have otherwise imagined. By now you know each person is different, they have their own unique crackhead, their own set of "tools" in their "toolbox" and will handle situations in a different way to you. That is why it is hard to find like-minded people, but when we do, we tend to keep them close as we perceive that we're "wired" the same. When we come into conflict with other people, it can be because our thinking patterns are not the same. So the next time you are in an argument with someone, or somebody does something in a different way to you, remind yourself they have a different crackhead, they have a different toolbox.

Rio and Kaiya have both learnt that not all relationships are supposed to last, and this is true for all of us. The problem is because we have so much emotional investment in our relationships when they end – either through break up, death, or even expectations not being met – it can become an all-you-can-eat-buffet for our crackhead. Some people can't stop thinking about that event, along with all its subtleties. Should I have done this? Where were you? Why did I react like that? All of these thoughts and impressions can be etched within our minds when some event, big or small, affects us in a way we don't like. The more you try to not think about it, the more you reinforce the thought process, which only helps to make it stronger in its ability to affect you and your natural way of thinking. The event only happened once, but it is your memory that is making you die a thousand deaths and only you have the power to stop that.

Rejection

This now brings me on to the concept of rejection:

> Rejection is something that everybody has to go through in life, but whether we let it affect us and who we are is our choice. "Areas of the brain appear to respond to the pain of rejection in the same way as physical pain," which is why it hurts so much. "Going back 50,000 years, social distance from a group could lead to death, and it still does for most infant mammals."[32] This is why the fear and the feeling of rejection is so painful for us as it is a warning mechanism; however, in today's day and age, if we get rejected it will no longer kill us, but our brain still registers it in the same original way.

We all experience the fear of rejection in different shapes and forms, but even though it may hurt, it won't kill us. It is just how our brain processes this information, and by understanding this, it allows us to become more aware of not only ourselves but how everybody else functions too. Now that you know your brain automatically does this, it will make it easier to accept and move through rejection.

Think about whether you have any thought patterns that cause you to behave in a certain way (for example, jealousy). When you can own that, which essentially means you can accept it, it allows you to forgive yourself and no longer be invested in

---

32 "Rejection Really Hurts", *Science Daily*, *2003*:
https://www.sciencedaily.com/releases/2003/10/031010074045.htm

the other person. Kaiya had to forgive herself because she felt guilty for not spending enough time with Ashley, and in doing so, she was able to let go and move on.

Remember, getting over somebody takes time. Not only does the relationship end, but so do all the future expectations you have. The loss of expectations in itself can be like dealing with a break-up as you saw with Rio. Never let anybody tell you how long it should take you to get over a relationship. They were not in the relationship. You were. There is no set time that it should take you to get over your ex. They have no idea of your level of emotional investment and how attached you became. A break-up is similar to a death because it is perceived as a loss in our minds. Anything, where we lose, takes time to recover from due to us placing attachment onto it. You should be kind to yourself in those periods, but you must also be smart. You have probably heard the expression "Everything becomes easier with time." If you don't deal with the issues from the last relationship, or life experience that has had an effect on you, it can and most likely will appear again in another shape or form. You saw how this type of thinking affected Kaiya's relationship with her mother. If you don't do the work and only rely on time, it will come back to bite you on your arse.

Your crackhead WILL most likely make things worse for you. It will create a number of convoluted scenarios that may never have existed or amplify ones. Below is an exercise on forgiveness that can help you through this process of loss, but at the same time you should also be kind to yourself and accept it may be challenging ahead, but you can get through it.

Exercise: Forgiveness

Forgiveness, letting go, and acceptance are important in maintaining your mental health and to stop you from beating yourself up about events that can no longer be changed.

1. Write down everything you haven't been able to forgive yourself for.

2. Ask yourself what it is you feel guilty about.

3. Why do you feel guilty about it? Remember sometimes these things just happen in your life, there are things you cannot control.

4. Start by saying, "I cannot change what has happened. I choose to accept what has happened is in the past. I am moving forward. I forgive myself."

5. You can also use the acceptance exercise on page 157 to help you with this.

6. Finally take ten deep breaths. With every inhale think of a colour, a colour which for you represents the colour of forgiveness. Every time you inhale imagine your body being filled with that colour until your entire body is now glowing in whatever this may be. Every time you exhale feel the guilt leaving your body. Imagine this as another colour and let it leave your body.

You may need to repeat this process more than once, but the more time you give yourself, the better. The more forgiveness you inhale and actually allow into your life, the more you will begin to move through whatever it is that you're dealing with.

Vishen Lakhiani, in *The Code of the Extraordinary Mind*,[33] talks about learning to fulfil yourself from an internal reservoir instead of becoming reliant on your partner or a goal. Learning to move toward a goal or be deeply in love with someone

---

33 Vishen Lakhiani. (2016). *Code of the Extraordinary Mind* (Rodale Books); pp.175–200.

without attaching yourself. He explains that our fear is not necessarily losing the other person but the part of ourselves that feels when we are with this person, a result of attaching your emotions to an external source. We saw this in the way that both Kaiya and Rio attached themselves to expectations and other people, and you saw what happened. If you have been through any form of relationship ending (does not have to be romantic) ask yourself:

- Did you allow certain thoughts or insecurities to take control in your head? For example, Rio felt he wasn't good enough, so always had to overcompensate. Kaiya didn't want to get hurt, so she tried to control everything.

- Did your preconceived ideas lead you to behave in a certain way? For example, being cool or playing games because you think the other person might leave you or get too comfortable if you show too much affection?

- Did you stop yourself from being honest and open due to feeling emotionally vulnerable? For example, you may have not wanted to open up fully because of a previous relationship or feel emotionally vulnerable.

These thoughts could have created behavioural patterns without you even realising. If you believe that you were fine with everything and it was something else, such as long distance that ended the relationship, then look at all the good memories you had and be grateful. Be glad you were able to fully live and experience that relationship. By not dealing with past emotions, you will carry them forward. This is another way of looking at what happens if you avoid your emotions or don't deal with your shit.

Exercise: Breaking the Hurdles

1. Imagine that you are running on a circular running track. It's just you. The crackhead may pop up and run beside you when they feel like it, but otherwise, it's just you. Now life decides to put a hurdle in your way. A hurdle can be any form of life lesson, relationship, job, etc. Your instinct may be to jump the hurdle and continue running, but at some point, or another when you run back around the track, the hurdle will still be there. The hurdle will now just appear in a different shape or experience in your life but still create the same emotions as before.

2. What should you be doing? You should be breaking the hurdle. Get a hammer, a chainsaw, some TNT, C4, whatever it may be but break that thing down. How do you do that in real life?

3. You start by asking yourself the questions given above, and getting honest about what you're avoiding, what you're running away from.

4. If you can't explain it, then think of a time you didn't like. Look at how it makes your body react and how you feel. Now write down and describe that feeling. Then slowly build up from there. You'll be amazed at actually how good you can become at understanding yourself.

When you learn to break life's hurdles and not to jump them, that's when you start dealing with them straight away no matter what. You go in with the mindset to learn, you understand that you should not put any expectations on it and no matter what the outcome is, you are going to do your very best every moment of the way. If you can do that, then you will be able to walk to your own beat and deal with anything life decides to test you with.

— 5 —

Push vs Pull

In the last section of Part I, Rio spoke about using a calendar as a way to remind himself of how far he had come. He spoke about how it created the same emotional attachment an addict gets from receiving their thirty days, sixty days, a hundred days chip. Your calendar can do exactly that for you. The *Beeja* app is free to download, has a timer and calendar stored within the app. This will allow you to keep track of how many days you meditate but also the number of hours you start to accumulate. This is the app I have personally found to be the most useful and practical.

It only takes a small amount of time to change something unfamiliar (i.e., maintaining your meditation and a healthy diet plan) for it to become familiar. The psychology behind changing habits, is that in the beginning, while these tasks may feel like "push tasks" (you have to motivate yourself to do them) eventually after a week, ten days, two weeks, and then a month especially, they start transforming from "push" to "pull." You are reminding yourself continuously of the emotional investment you have put into something every day, and you then begin to think really hard about whether or not you want to break your streak.

Convert Push to Pull Objectives

Anything in your life that you have to push yourself towards requires lots of willpower and motivation. This tool allows you to convert push to pull objectives. Pull objectives means you are naturally inclined to do it as the task is pulling you to do it. You want to. You begin to enjoy the process a lot more, and what is the by-product? The results you have wanted.

David Eagleman, a renowned neuroscientist, said: *"To the brain, the future can only ever be a pale shadow of now. The power of now explains why people make decisions that feel good at the moment but have lousy consequences in the future."*[34]

This tool helps you become accountable and reduces the temptation and power of now. The more you build up, the more your brain gets wired in not giving into temptation. It also highlights how something so simple can start creating habits of success. The first week, sometimes the second, is usually the hardest, but once you get over those hurdles you'll find you start being pulled to your goals. You do not have to continuously start something new, but the by-products of falling in love with daily habits have been the following for me:

- Reduced fear and anxiety of the future

- Increased self-confidence and self-love

- Reduced the noise of the crackhead – doesn't speak anywhere near as much as previously

- Reduction in body fat percentage

- The ability to stay calmer in unexpected situations that life will throw at you, e.g., job or romantic rejections (this is always a work in progress and you should only look at where you used to be and compare that to where you are now)

---

34 David Eagleman (2015) *The Brain: The Story of You* (Canongate Books Ltd); p.131.

- Increase in all-round mental well-being and daily happiness

Find what works for you, and the only way to do that is by trying new things. This tool has been the simplest, but most effective in my personal development so far. My hope is that by the end of all of this, you can be your own renewable source of self-love and acceptance which means you will be "getting high on your own supply."[35]

---

35 Wim Hof – creator of the Wim Hof Method

— 6 —

Your Purpose

Up to this point everything I have explained has been around getting to the root of your problems, how to bounce back from curve balls and how to maintain a state of equilibrium. But what do you do next? Once you're at the point where you're loving life and feeling content, what is the other part of the puzzle that has not been spoken about? That question is, *What is my purpose?*

Discovering what your true purpose is, helps you become the best version of yourself. It allows your avatar to upgrade to its maximum potential and who wouldn't want that? After all we only get one.

You've probably been asked, what do you want to do when you're older? Where do you see yourself in five years? What career do you want? Growing up in the digital age with so much access to the quantum of information we have, means we can do just about anything now, but this can be a double-edged sword for those who do not know what to do and don't know how to find out what truly resonates with their true sense of self. For some, this question can make you panic, freeze, cause avoidance because we don't know what we want which is infuriating but also not knowing, how to know what we want, makes things ten times worse.

This now brings me onto something called your ikigai. Ikigai is a Japanese concept for your life's purpose. Finding your ikigai will help turn you into a guided missile that will manoeuvre and meander like water around any obstacle but will help you ultimately hit your final target. Your ikigai is the central point of what you love doing, what you are good at, what the world needs and what you can be paid for.

Gay Hendricks, author of *The Big Leap*, has a great technique called "The Russian Doll" which for those of you who may find the ikigai questions too difficult to answer, I highly recommend looking into it.

Here is how I look at it, but before you continue to the exercise please bear this in mind. Forget about what society and social norms tells you that you should like. Your purpose is about you and what resonates with you at the highest vibration. For some people chasing money is their ikigai. For others, it is helping people. Put your phone away, give yourself some time to think and don't be frustrated if you don't get these answers straight away. They can take time to form and they can adapt and morph gradually over time as you move through different stages of your life, but know there will be some similarities and patterns you have enjoyed doing the most. When you discover those know you're looking in the right area.

Exercise: Life Purpose

1. Describe your perfect workday.

2. What skills are you demonstrating during the day? (Think of what your passion is. Look at the skills involved in said passion.) For example, I'm creating new products or services with a team. I'm innovating and building something with my mind and my hands. I'm learning at the same time. I'm meeting new people and not only building a product/service that people enjoy using, but I am able to connect with them.

3. What other activities are you doing?

4. For example, I'm able to go to the gym/play some form of recreational sport. Spend time with my family/partner. Go to an amazing restaurant (I love Roka and their wagyu steak, so in my perfect day, I get to have this for dinner). Have sex with the partner I love (again be as open and candid as you can be).

5. How much are you earning (to make it easier put down your yearly income)?

6. This question can be hard for people, and it really highlights what people think their true value is. Put down a number you think that you genuinely deserve and believe with your whole heart. Remember just because you do not have the skills now to achieve this number, does not mean you won't have them in the future. Don't get bogged down in thinking how you'll learn these skills, just believe you will get to a point where you have them and you're earning what you want to earn.

Once you have spent time doing all of this look at your week and carve out "soul time." Soul time is where you spend an hour, thirty minutes, a whole day, whatever it is, devoted to pursuing your ikigai while still maintaining your day-to-day life. That job you're currently working in that you may not enjoy all of a sudden takes on a new role; A source of income for you while you build ikigai and something that can help finance your true destination. Sticking to your soul time is the hard bit, as this is the time that people tend to sacrifice when life gets in the way, but this soul time is as important for you as therapy, working on your mental health, or going to the gym. The more you put into your soul time the more you'll get out of it and you'll start to see shifts in the way you think and feel about your purpose. You will start to feel like you have some direction if you didn't otherwise, you may have more clarity about what it is specifically you want to do, or better yet you may decide to take the plunge to pursue your ikigai through and through with 100 per cent commitment. The beautiful thing is once you find the different aspects of your ikigai, if something enters your life that doesn't suit it, you may very well choose not to let it penetrate your life space.

Thank you so much for picking up this book. I hope you have been able to take away something from it and enjoyed reading it as much as I did going through this journey of writing it. If there is only one thing you take away from this, take this: change your thoughts, change your reality.

— 7 —

The Fifty-Day Crackhead Challenge

By now, you will know Rio and Kaiya undertook several practices and ways to improve their crackhead's state. The question is, would you like to do the same? Below outlines a reboot you can try for your mind. Think of it as a software update. Start by making a note of your intended start and finish dates. Then for the following fifty days, take the time to focus on the internal and forget the external by using the following guidelines.

The Rules

From **Day 1** onwards you will be required to do the following:

No Social Media

Deactivate your social media accounts (this means nobody can find you on social media) and then delete the apps from your phone, including Facebook, Instagram, Tik Tok, LinkedIn, Twitter, Snapchat, and so on. Remember, all of your closest friends who you truly care about will have your mobile number. They can WhatsApp/text/call you if you want to organise anything with them.

Meditation

Start a daily meditation or breathing exercise practice for a minimum of ten minutes. Ideally, do your practice in the morning before breakfast and your caffeine hit/cigarette if you smoke.

From **Day 5** onwards you will be required to do the following:

Phone Diary

Keep a notes page on your phone and write a journal – daily if you can. The aim here is to record all of your emotions when you feel like quitting or want to stop. Also, take a note of your energy levels. More often than not, when you are tired/fatigued, your emotions go haywire. Hormonal issues can also be an issue so be mindful of that. It doesn't need to be too detailed. For example:

08/11/2020 – Recovering from COVID-19. Energy levels very low. Feel tired/bored/lethargic. crackhead is pretty calm. Feel stuck but will do some CFA work to flex brain muscles to remove the feeling

15/11/2020 – Feeling amazing. Worked out, ate clean, meditated. Emotions and energy at the top level.

From **Day 14** onwards you will be required to do the following:

Fitness

Create a sustainable workout plan that you can stick to. Something manageable. For me it was three times a week but whatever you decide on you are making a commitment to yourself to stick to it. You need to do something more than once a week. (Regardless of any health issues you may or may not have check with your physician before starting any new exercise regime.)

For example, on Monday, Wednesday, Friday I would do HIIT (high-intensity interval training) or go for a run. Do something for a minimum of thirty minutes to get your heart rate elevated and your endorphins going. Remember the endorphin hit will make you feel good and reduce the crackhead, and if you're in shape, you naturally feel more confident.

Eating
Cut out one bad thing for the next thirty-six days: chocolate, sugar, fizzy drinks, takeaways. You are not going to starve yourself, but a rule of thumb is to increase your protein and healthy fats and reduce your carbohydrate intake. If you are in a calorie deficit, you will also begin to lose weight. What you put into your body is so important as it affects how you feel. (Seek the guidance of a nutritionist if you want to get a real break down of what to do. It was one of the best investments I made into myself. Again speak to your physician before starting any diet plan)

From **Day 30** onwards you will be required to do the following:

Tapes
Use the "changing your language exercise". Don't forget to record yourself saying everything. Say it slowly so you can hear every word you're saying and say it with 100 per cent conviction and determination (that doesn't mean you have to shout). Go through your list at least three times, you want the tape to be at least five minutes long. Play this recording every night as you fall asleep or set it as your alarm so it is the first thing you hear when you wake up in the morning.

Ikigai
Go back to Section 6 in Part II and carry out the exercise designed to help you understand what is your purpose, your ikigai, your north star. Take your time working on this and let yourself ponder on it. Go back to it after a week and see how

you feel about your answers. If you should feel so inclined then start implementing some soul time into your life too and make a commitment to yourself that you will do so. Write it down on a piece of paper and stick it on your ceiling above your bed so every day when you wake up and before you go to bed you remember that commitment you have made to yourself.

Sleep
Try to go to bed and get up every day at approximately the same time and ensure you get eight hours of restful sleep.

Optional

- **Reading:** Read one book over the next fifty days that will help change your mindset. It can be anything with regards to self-development.

- **Fresh Air:** Try and go for a twenty to thirty-minute walk/ run on your lunch break. Go outside, don't call anyone, listen to music, walk and take deep breaths of the fresh air. Focus on your breath and creating a calming feeling.

- **Sex:** If you really want a challenge, abstain from sex and any form of masturbation. This is completely down to you, but the reasoning behind this is that the extra energy you gain from abstaining you can then use on your workouts, reading, or anything to make yourself better. Also, if you watch porn during either of these activities, it gives your mind a mental cleanse from it all.

Milestones

Keep a note of the following milestones: days one, five, seven, ten, fourteen, twenty-one, thirty, forty, forty-nine, fifty. This way, you can continuously look at the next milestone and know you're never too far away from achieving it – especially on the days you feel like quitting. Keep getting to the next milestone and celebrate the small victories on the way (that doesn't mean eating a cheat meal every milestone day to celebrate).

Checklists

Use the following checklists to help you launch your challenge and stay on track:

Day 1 Checklist

- Delete social media accounts.

- Put the calendar widget on your phone home screen and make it the whole page. This should be the first thing you see when you look at your phone. Find a symbol you can put into the calendar, like a tick or any form of emoji that reminds you that you have completed everything you had to for that day. This will help change push actions to pull actions and remind you of the time and sacrifice you have put in to do everything for yourself.

- Look at what type of meditation you want to try.

Enjoy the journey.

I would love to hear if this book has helped you in any way, so feel free to send a message to crackheadconversations@gmail.com and let me know how you got on or any other thoughts you may have.

Resources

Eagleman, D. (2015). *The Brain: The Story of You*. (Canongate Book Ltd).

Singer, M. (2007). *The Untethered Soul*. (Yellow Kite Books).

Lakhiani, V. (2016). Code of the Extraordinary Mind. (Rodale Books).

Katherine Woodward Thomas – Conscious Uncoupling Masterclass on Mindvalley https://www.mindvalley.com/conscious-uncoupling/masterclass?utm_source=google

Beeja Meditation Website: https://www.beejameditation.com/?utm_term=beeja&utm_source=google&utm_medium=cpc&utm_campaign=Brand_Exact&gclid=Cj0KCQjwjoH0BRD6ARIsAEWO9Dsm_TgXL7BWF9iQuvFVe2sXfe0u4Vx5zgPRZzikAiZYLkHao0oxKIsaAkShEALw_wcB

Headspace Meditation: https://www.headspace.com/?utm_source=google&utm_medium=cpc&utm_campaign=917256451&utm_content=51529951612&utm_term=411021410531&headspace&gclid=Cj0KCQjwjoH0BRD6ARIsAEWO9Ds905THKoHd6g93Q0rxQmHDg9Yw5edB2MiKwwYZEpGpL8c0cm0b-D8aAtcCEALw_wcB

Sciencedaily (2003) – "Rejection Really Hurts. https://www.sciencedaily.com/releases/2003/10/031010074045.htm

Mindvalley website: https://www.mindvalley.com/

The Wellness Enterprise (2021) - https://thewellnessenterprise.com/emoto/

Acknowledgements

Mum and Dad. Words cannot express how grateful I will forever be for everything you have done for me. You are the best parents anyone could have ever asked for and I hope when it's my time to be a parent, I will be able to be half the human being the two of you are. Lil Sis, I want you to know how incredibly proud I am of you too. Everything you have been through, how you've matured and grown, you are one of the people that motivates me to be better.

Special thanks to Saint Allives, Ria Manna, Erima Longsig & Sandy Draper, four people who were instrumental in helping me turn this vision into reality. Thank you for all of your help.

Finally, I'd also like to give a shout out to Jan Liloham, Jagem Nagsavi, Marty Simir, Muken Currar, Tan Rzenksk, Sivahe Vadiamma, Dalgoud McGoualld, Karl Maces, and Raz Cark people who have helped me learn and made me laugh on so many occasions for many years and hopefully many years to come. Thank you for everything, my life genuinely wouldn't have been the same without you.

NEW RELEASE

Check out the album inspired by this book on Spotify & Apple Music to be released in the latter part of 2022 by the artist known as "The ProfessR".

Lightning Source UK Ltd.
Milton Keynes UK
UKHW010626230622
404860UK00001B/238